POTTER V. SHRACKLE
AND
THE SHRACKLE CONSTRUCTION COMPANY

Eighth Edition

Case File

Trial Materials

POTTER V. SHRACKLE
AND
THE SHRACKLE CONSTRUCTION COMPANY

Eighth Edition

Case File

Trial Materials

Kenneth S. Broun
Henry Brandis Professor of Law Emeritus
University of North Carolina School of Law

Frank D. Rothschild
Attorney at Law
Kilauea, Hawaii

Revision by Kenneth S. Broun and Frank D. Rothschild based upon the
original file created by Kenneth S. Broun as revised by James H. Seckinger

NATIONAL INSTITUTE FOR TRIAL ADVOCACY

Address inquiries to:
Reprint Permission
National Institute for Trial Advocacy
325 W. South Boulder Rd., Ste. 1
Louisville, CO 80027–1130
Phone: (800) 225-6482
Email: permissions@nita.org

ISBN 978-1-60156-991-2
FBA 1991
eISBN 978-1-60156-992-9
FBA1992

Printed in the United States of America

Official co-publisher of NITA.
WKLegaledu.com/NITA

CONTENTS

Acknowledgments

The authors would like to thank the following for their assistance in the creation of the photographs and video clips that come with this file: Craig Gilbert, general contractor (Charles Shrackle); Bobby Dudley, former contractor and now Kona lawyer (Jeffrey Potter); Bob Bissenette, commercial painter (James Marshall); Courtney Haas, realtor and yoga instructor (Cheryl Tobias); and especially Anne Slifkin, attorney and mediator, whose portrayal of Kathy Potter in the original version of this file (c. 1976) became part of NITA lore.

We are also deeply indebted to Juan Gonzalez III, Principal, and Jaime Jue, Senior Associate, in the forensic department of KPMG LLP for their outstanding work in upgrading and enriching the experts portion of this file, including the reports and tables of Dr. Glenn and Dr. Buchanan, the Dyer memorandum, and other related materials.

INTRODUCTION

This is a wrongful death action brought in Nita State Court by Jeffrey T. Potter, as administrator of the estate of his deceased wife, Katherine, and in his own behalf, against Charles T. Shrackle and the Shrackle Construction Company. Potter claims that Shrackle negligently drove the company's pickup, striking Katherine Potter as she was crossing the street, causing her death. Potter claims that Shrackle was acting in the course of the Shrackle Construction Company's business at the time of the accident.

Shrackle admits striking Ms. Potter, but claims that she was crossing in the middle of the street, rather than in the pedestrian crosswalk, and that she did not look before entering the street in the path of Mr. Shrackle's truck. Defendants deny that Shrackle was negligent and allege contributory negligence on the part of the deceased, Ms. Potter.

Electronic versions of all exhibits and the PowerPoint presentation are available for download at

http://bit.ly/1P20Jea
Password is Potter8

IN THE CIRCUIT COURT OF
DARROW COUNTY, NITA
CIVIL DIVISION

Jeffrey T. Potter, the	)	
Administrator of the Estate	)	
of Katherine Potter, and	)	
Jeffrey T. Potter, individually,	)	
	)	Complaint
Plaintiffs,	)	
	)	
v.	)	
	)	
Charles T. Shrackle and	)	
The Shrackle Construction Company,	)	
	)	
Defendants.	)	

Plaintiff, Jeffrey T. Potter, individually and as administrator of the Estate of Katherine Potter, complains against Defendants, Charles T. Shrackle and Shrackle Construction Company, as follows:

FIRST CLAIM FOR RELIEF

1. Plaintiff was, and still is, a resident of Darrow County, Nita.

2. Defendant Charles T. Shrackle was, and still is, a resident of Darrow County, Nita, and the Defendant Shrackle Construction Company was, and still is, doing business in Darrow County, Nita.

3. Katherine Potter died on December 4, 2021.

4. Plaintiff and Katherine Potter were married at the time of her death and had been married for twelve years.

5. Plaintiff has been duly appointed the Administrator of Katherine Potter's estate.

6. On November 30, 2021, at about 3:30 p.m., Katherine Potter was walking in an easterly direction across Mattis Avenue at the intersection of Mattis and Kirby Avenues in Nita City, Nita.

7. At this time and place Defendant Charles T. Shrackle was driving a 2007 Toyota pickup truck, which struck Katherine Potter, causing her serious injuries and death as a result of such injuries on December 4, 2021.

8. The truck driven by Defendant Charles T. Shrackle was owned by the Defendant Shrackle Construction Company, and at the time Katherine Potter was struck by the truck, Charles T. Shrackle was performing duties for and acting on behalf of the Shrackle Construction Company.

9. Defendant Charles T. Shrackle was driving the Toyota pickup truck in a careless, negligent, and reckless manner, and in violation of his duties under Nita Revised Statutes 89-12(4) (2021) to exercise due care to avoid striking the pedestrian Katherine Potter who was then lawfully walking across the street.

10. Defendant Charles T. Shrackle carelessly, negligently, and in violation of Nita Revised Statutes 89-12(4)(2021) failed to keep a proper lookout, to heed the fact that Katherine Potter was crossing the street in the immediate path of his truck, or to take any action to avoid striking Katherine Potter.

11. Defendant Charles T. Shrackle carelessly, negligently, and in violation of Nita Revised Statutes 89-12(4)(2021) failed to give proper warning of the sudden and unexpected approach of his truck either by sounding the horn or giving any other signal or warning.

12. Defendant Charles T. Shrackle's negligence caused Katherine Potter to suffer severe physical and mental pain and suffering from the date such injuries were incurred on November 30, 2021, until her death on December 4, 2021.

13. Defendant Charles T. Shrackle's negligence caused Katherine Potter to incur reasonable expenses for medical, hospital, and surgical care, and the loss of wages from the time of the collision until her death, in the sum of $107,800.

14. Defendant Charles T. Shrackle's negligence caused Jeffrey T. Potter, as personal representative of the Estate of Katherine Potter, to incur reasonable funeral and burial expenses, in the sum of $16,500.

SECOND CLAIM FOR RELIEF

15. Plaintiff realleges paragraphs 1 through 11.

16. Defendant Charles T. Shrackle's negligence caused Jeffrey T. Potter, as the surviving spouse of Katherine Potter, to suffer damages for the loss of:

    (a) The reasonable expected net income of Katherine Potter;

    (b) Services, protection, care, and assistance of Katherine Potter, whether voluntary or obligatory, to Jeffrey T. Potter;

    (c) Society, companionship, comfort, guidance, kindly offices, and advice of Katherine Potter to Jeffrey T. Potter.

WHEREFORE, Plaintiff demands judgment against Defendants, jointly and severally, in an amount in excess of $50,000, together with interest thereon and his costs herein, and for such other relief as the Court deems just and proper.

JURY DEMAND

Plaintiff demands a trial by jury in this action.

MADDEN & JAMES

by

William James

Attorneys for Plaintiff

Suite 720, Nita Bank Building

Nita City, Nita 99994

(555) 555-0003

DATED: November 2, 2022

IN THE CIRCUIT COURT OF
DARROW COUNTY, NITA
CIVIL DIVISION

Jeffrey T. Potter, the)
Administrator of the Estate)
of Katherine Potter, and)
Jeffrey T. Potter, individually,)
)   Answer
Plaintiffs,.)
)
v.)
)
Charles T. Shrackle and)
The Shrackle Construction Company,)
)
Defendants.)

Defendants for their Answer to Plaintiff's Complaint:

1. Admit the allegations contained in paragraphs 1–5, 7–8.

2. Admit that on November 30, 2021, at or about 3:30 p.m., Katherine Potter was crossing Mattis Avenue somewhere near the intersection of Kirby and Mattis Avenues. Defendants deny all other allegations in paragraph 6.

3. Deny the allegations contained in paragraphs 9–14, 16.

FIRST AFFIRMATIVE DEFENSE

4. Any injuries sustained or suffered by Katherine Potter at the time and place mentioned in the Complaint were caused, in whole or in part, or were contributed to, by the negligence of Katherine Potter and not by any negligence of Charles T. Shrackle.

SECOND AFFIRMATIVE DEFENSE

5. Katherine Potter violated Nita Revised Statutes 89-12(4)(2021) by failing to cross the street in the marked pedestrian crosswalk, to keep a proper lookout for vehicles using the roadway, and to yield the right of way to any such vehicles.

WHEREFORE, Defendants demand that judgment be entered in favor of the Defendants with the costs and disbursements of this action.

PIERCE, JOHNSON & CLARK

by

James Barber

Attorneys for Defendants

Nita National Bank Plaza

Nita City, Nita 99994

(555) 555-6207

DATED: December 1, 2022

PLAINTIFF'S DEPOSITIONS

SUMMARY OF DEPOSITION OF MARILYN J. KELLY

My name is Marilyn J. Kelly. I live at 1910 Elder Lane, Nita City 99992.

On November 30, 2021, I was driving my car on Mattis Avenue, traveling northeast toward Kirby Avenue. I was in the right lane of traffic, closest to the east side of the street. At approximately 3:20 p.m., I was stopped for a red light at the intersection of Mattis and Kirby Avenues. I was first in line and was stopped just south of the crosswalk.

As I came to a stop, a young boy ran across Mattis from the west to east. I gasped as a car making a left turn from Kirby onto Mattis slammed on its brakes and barely avoided hitting him. When he reached the sidewalk, the crossing guard who was standing on the southeast corner of the intersection yelled at the boy—something to the effect of, "You need to watch for cars."

I looked back to the corner where the boy had run across the street. That's when I saw a woman with dark hair dressed in a dark jacket with some color on it and a dark skirt on the west side of Mattis Avenue. I watched her step off the curb and start crossing the street. The woman was walking at a normal gait and was not running. She was definitely in the crosswalk, and I saw her take two or three steps.

I had just glanced back up at the light when I heard a thud. I looked toward that noise and saw the woman fly through the air with her arms outstretched and land on the front of the truck. She fell backward off the hood, as if doing a backward somersault, and fell under the truck. She didn't complete a somersault, but just flew back and landed with her head smashing on the pavement. I thought, "My God, stop, don't run over her again." The truck driver craned his neck from side to side immediately after the impact as though looking to see what he had hit.

The truck stopped at a point approximately forty feet south of the south line of Kirby. At the point where the truck stopped, the woman was almost entirely underneath the truck. I definitely heard the thud before I heard the sound of any brakes shrieking. At the time of the thud the front of the truck was about even with the front of my car and was not completely straightened out from making the left turn.

The sun at the time of the occurrence was extremely bright and low in the sky, coming from a southwesterly direction. I had to shade my eyes when I looked back to the scene after the truck came to a stop.

After the truck stopped, a man ran out from the car wash across the street, and the driver of the truck got out and went around to the front of his truck. I thought that the guy driving the truck was Charles Shrackle, but I wasn't sure at the time.

I stayed at the scene for a couple of minutes, and then I left and went to my appointment with my firm's accountant in the Lincolnshire Shopping Plaza. My appointment was at 3:30 p.m.

Lincolnshire is about a fifteen-minute drive from Kirby and Mattis. I was particularly concerned about the time because traffic had been heavy that day as I came up Mattis. The schools were getting out just as I was traveling on Mattis. What ordinarily would be a ten-minute trip for me took me close to twenty-five minutes.

I am thirty-seven years old. I work as the office manager of a local construction company, Buildit. Although I don't know Charles Shrackle well, I know his business is a competitor of our company. I have met him at some Builders Association meetings. Frankly, I don't like him much. He has always seemed arrogant—somebody who's always in a hurry to get to the top. It's funny that he is so ambitious because I don't think his company is doing that well. We took over one school construction job from them a year or so ago when the school district was unhappy with the progress of the work.

The following morning after I got to work, I read about the accident in the online edition of the Nita City newspaper. The newspaper article said that the woman was running and was approximately thirty feet south of the crosswalk at the time she was hit by the truck. They got it all wrong. I told my boss, Susannah Bond, about it. Susannah said I should call the police and tell them what I saw. So I called the police and advised them that I had witnessed the accident, and that the woman was in the crosswalk and not running at all.

After I hung up, Susannah and I talked about Shrackle. Susannah told me about Shrackle's problems on the Greenbriar job. She said she had chatted with Clark Poe, the general contractor on that job. She told me there was some possibility we were going to take over that Greenbriar project if Shrackle didn't get his act together.

I did not know Katherine Potter, nor do I know Jeffrey Potter or anyone else in their family.

I have read the foregoing and it is a true and accurate transcription of my deposition testimony given on January 12, 2023.

Signed: *Marilyn J. Kelly*   Date: January 12, 2023

Marilyn J. Kelly
Subscribed and sworn to before me this 12th day of January, 2023.

Lucy Madison

Lucy Madison
Notary

SUMMARY OF DEPOSITION OF MICHAEL YOUNG

I am Michael Young. I am a police officer for the Nita Police Department and have been on the police force for seven years. My duties have consisted largely of general patrol duty during that time. I was assigned to patrol duty on November 30, 2021.

The afternoon of November 30 was clear, the sun was shining. The pavement was dry. There had not been rain for several days. Exhibit 25 is the report from the Nita City Weather Bureau's website that I printed out for that day. I remember later, at the scene of the accident, that I thought that the sun was particularly bright that late fall day. At 3:28 that afternoon, I was dispatched to the scene of an accident in which a pedestrian had been struck by a vehicle. I was only a few blocks away, on the corner of Greenview and Whitehead Road, and got there within about two minutes. The accident occurred on Mattis Avenue, just south of Kirby. Mattis is a four-lane road at that point with two lanes in either direction. There is a three-foot-wide concrete median separating the north- and southbound lanes. Exhibit 14 is a photo of that median from where it starts at the intersection looking southwest. Exhibit 15 shows the same median looking back up toward Kirby.

When I arrived at the scene, I found the victim, who I later identified as Katherine Potter, age forty-five, lying underneath a pickup truck. Charles T. Shrackle, age thirty-eight, identified himself as the driver of the truck. I asked Mr. Shrackle to move the truck back so that I could aid Ms. Potter. He did so. Ms. Potter was alive and appeared to be conscious. She was moaning and there was a grimace on her face. She appeared to be in a lot of pain. Her eyes were closed for the most part, but she opened them several times. She didn't seem to focus on me or anything else. At one point, it sounded like she said the name "Jeff." She said it maybe three or four times in a row. She didn't say anything else. I saw no indication that Ms. Potter or Mr. Shrackle had used alcohol or any other intoxicating substance.

The photograph, Exhibit 4, is a fair and accurate depiction of Ms. Potter as she lay on the pavement before the ambulance arrived and after the truck was backed away.

I waited with Ms. Potter until the ambulance arrived. After the ambulance took her away, I began in earnest to conduct an investigation. I talked with some other witnesses at the scene, including Jim Marshall and Ed Putnam, who work at the car wash. I also talked to Mr. Shrackle. He told me that he had turned left onto Mattis from Kirby. He said that he felt an impact after he passed the curb south of Kirby Avenue. He remembered that the impact was several seconds after he passed the curb. He didn't know what had happened, but that he took his foot from the accelerator and put it on the brake as hard and quickly as he could. He was able to stop the truck and got out and found Ms. Potter lying underneath it.

I took measurements of the location of the truck after Ms. Potter was taken away by the ambulance. The measurements are indicated on my police report. I had Mr. Shrackle move the truck back to the place that it had been, or at least as close as we could figure it was. I measured the distance as fifty-two feet, four inches from the beginning of the crosswalk for pedestrians crossing Mattis on the south side of Kirby. The crosswalk is approximately five feet wide and the limit line on the east side of Mattis is another three feet down from the crosswalk. There were almost seventeen feet of skid marks up to the place where the truck was stopped. These measurements are all on my police accident report, Exhibit 1, which I made as part of my official duties. Based upon the formula that we use, the skid marks would tell us that the truck's minimum speed at the time of the impact would have been thirty-three miles per hour.

No, I haven't taken the accident reconstruction courses offered by the department yet, but I got the thirty-three miles an hour based on this formula they gave us to help estimate speed. No, I don't know whether the formula changes with the type of vehicle. It's just a general formula, I think.

Based on my investigation, I concluded that no citations were justified. Based on that investigation and my experience, I concluded that Ms. Potter was out of the crosswalk when she was hit. She was probably fifteen to twenty feet south of the crosswalk at the point of impact.

I took the photographs labeled Exhibits 9–21 about a week after Katherine Potter died. I took them as part of my continuing investigation and at the request of the district attorney's office. I started taking photos of various views of the intersection of Kirby and Mattis Avenues somewhere around 3:00 to 3:30 in the afternoon and they accurately show that intersection as it existed on the date of this tragic accident. I am not sure of the exact time I started taking pictures nor when I finished.

Exhibit 2 is a scale diagram of the intersection of Kirby and Mattis that I obtained from the Nita City Department of Public Works. Exhibit 2a identifies the location of the carwash and the White Castle. Exhibit 2b indicates the route witnesses reported that Katherine Potter was taking before she was hit. Exhibit 2c tracks the route of Mr. Shrackle's truck prior to hitting Ms. Potter. Exhibit 2d indicates the direction and distance to the Potters' home in relation to the accident site.

Exhibit 3 is an electronic blow-up of that same intersection showing the various crosswalks and medians. It is to scale. On Exhibits 3a through 3e, I placed letters representing the position at the time of the accident of each of the witnesses I interviewed. The photos marked as Exhibits 9–21 have arrows indicating where I was that point in the direction I was facing as I took each photo.

I have read the foregoing and it is a true and accurate transcription of my deposition testimony given on January 16, 2023.

Signed: *Michael Young*   Date: January 16, 2023

Michael Young

Subscribed and sworn before me this 16th day of January, 2023.

Harry Gibbons

Harry Gibbons

Notary

Summary of Deposition of James Marshall

I am the owner and operator of the car wash on Kirby where it intersects with Mattis, 1601 Kirby, Nita City, Nita. I have owned and operated the business for fifteen years.

I know Charles Shrackle. He has brought both his business and personal vehicles into my place for cleaning over the years. He's been a good customer. A good guy, too.

I was standing just outside the entrance to our office, which is on the wall facing the intersection, when I saw a dark-haired woman walking east on the south sidewalk of Kirby right in front of my shop. Exhibit 21 shows my car wash and the sidewalk this woman was walking along. I would have been standing behind the big car wash sign just outside the office entrance along that wall.

Page 17

Q. What time was this?

A. About 3:30 in the afternoon.

Q. What did you see?

A. When I first saw the dark-haired woman, she was maybe thirty feet from the intersection on the sidewalk.

Q. What did she look like?

A. I remember that she seemed to be in her forties or fifties, but I don't remember what she was wearing or much else about her.

Q. Then what happened?

A. About a minute or minute and a half later I heard a thump coming from the direction of Mattis Avenue. I ran out to the front of the car wash area and looked toward the spot where I had heard the thud. It was just south of the intersection on Mattis.

Q. Can you be more specific as to where that spot was?

A. I can't say for sure if the noise came from the area of the crosswalk or was south of it, but it was real close to that point. No more than five feet south of the crosswalk.

Q: Just to make sure, how long was it from the time you first saw the woman walking on the sidewalk until you heard the thud?

A: No more than a minute, maybe a minute and a half. I had been talking to a customer during that time.

Exhibit 13 shows my place across the street and the crosswalk Ms. Potter headed down, to-wards where the person taking this picture was standing.

When I looked in the direction of Mattis, I saw Mr. Shrackle's Toyota pickup carrying a body in front of it. I realized within a few moments that the truck was one of the Shrackle Construction Company trucks we had cleaned and detailed. You can't miss a Shrackle Construction vehicle with that logo he has on all the doors. I sent one of my employees to help and called 9-1-1 on my cell phone. I then went to help and saw that the injured woman was the same woman I had seen walking east on Kirby.

I stayed near her until the police arrived. I told the police the same thing I just told you. I also told all this to some guy from the insurance company who came to see me a couple of weeks after the accident.

Exhibit 9 shows the sidewalk outside my business looking east across Mattis towards the White Castle. Ms. Potter was in the shadow at the bottom of this picture when I first saw her.

Exhibit 22 is a statement this investigator fellow wrote up after talking to me a couple weeks after the accident. That's my signature at the bottom and initials at the top. He got a couple of things about me wrong. I think he asked me about those things specifically, so I changed them although I didn't really read the statement very carefully. The investigator was in a hurry to get someplace, so I looked it over real quick and signed it.

I have read the foregoing and it is a true and accurate transcription of my deposition testimony given on January 17, 2023.

Signed: Date: January 17, 2023

James Marshall

James Marshall

Subscribed and sworn before me this 17th day of January, 2023.

Harry Gibbons

Harry Gibbons

Notary

SUMMARY OF DEPOSITION OF JEFFREY T. POTTER

I am Jeffrey Potter, the plaintiff in this case. I live at 4920 Thorndale in Nita City in the same house that Katherine and I lived in before her death. I am forty-nine years of age. I'm a professor in the physics department at the University of Nita. I received a bachelor's degree in physics from Purdue and a doctorate in physics from the University of Wisconsin/Madison. I received my PhD twenty-four years ago and have been at the University of Nita since 1999.

Katherine and I were married twelve years ago, June 15, 2010. We met because we sang in the same community chorus. She was a high school computer science teacher then. She got a BS in computer science from Nita City University in 2003. She worked on her PhD in computer science from 2003 to 2005, but never finished. She had done all of her course work, but had not completed her dissertation. She told me she decided that she could accomplish more for herself and the world by teaching in high school and she didn't need a PhD to do that. But, by the time we met in 2009, she was disillusioned with teaching. She was tired of working as hard as you do as a high school teacher and not making much money.

Shortly after we got married, she left teaching and began working for Techno-Soft, Inc., a software company. She loved the work at Techno-Soft and was making a great deal more money. She became very ambitious in her career, but not so much that we didn't have a good time together. I was busy with my work as well, so our schedule and career goals were compatible.

Despite both of our involvement in our work, Katherine and I had other interests and spent a great deal of time together. We went to movies and out to dinner whenever we could. We also liked to sing with the community chorus. She had a beautiful alto voice; I am a so-so bass. We attended most the practices, which were once a week. The chorus performed concerts about four times a year and we would rehearse even more frequently as we got closer to concert time.

We also loved to travel, particularly to Europe. I had the summers free, and we used Katherine's yearly three-week vacation to travel. Tuscany and Umbria were our favorites. We loved to walk in the Italian countryside or have a glass of wine or coffee at a sidewalk cafe. We had a pretty special relationship until Shrackle took her life. I think we had about as near perfect a relationship as is possible in a marriage.

I did write the letter to Dr. Stevens marked Exhibit 28. As I said in the letter, I thought our marriage would work out just fine. Kathy and I, like most couples, had some difficulties over the years. She was always driven by her work, first teaching and then with Techno-Soft, and that was an ongoing problem. We also disagreed ultimately about having children. We tried to achieve a pregnancy early on in our marriage and had difficulties. After a lot of testing, the doctors couldn't identify a problem, but we still never conceived. I wanted to explore in vitro fertilization, and possibly adoption, but Kathy was opposed, so we resigned ourselves to our very comfortable life.

Around the time of Kathy's death, we were having a disagreement over retirement. I wanted Kathy to retire early so we could travel more, and she wanted to continue working. She was very ambitious. We were working through that problem with Dr. Stevens when Kathy was killed. Although it was a bone of contention, it did not threaten our marriage. I said in the letter that I might seek another relationship if our marriage didn't work out, but that was a remote possibility. We had always been able to work out our problems, whatever they were. No, I did not have another relationship in mind at that time or at any time during our marriage, and I resent your insinuation. I was completely faithful to Kathy and she to me. After Kathy died, I saw Dr. Stevens briefly, maybe three times, and he helped me with my grieving, but ultimately you have to learn to live with your loss. Time is the best healer.

Katherine had done well at Techno-Soft and they liked her. Despite the tough times for the software business, Techno-Soft has done fairly well.

Page 18

Q. How did Katherine like her work?

A. Techno-Soft gave her very interesting work projects, although she had to work long hours, and she certainly enjoyed making some real money after all those years in teaching.

Q. How did you feel about her work?

A. I liked the fact she found her work rewarding, but I thought she might want to take it easy and spend more time traveling.

Q. Had you talked to her about the possibility of retiring?

A. I had talked to her now and again about retiring and traveling with me during the summers. She seemed to be interested in the idea, but hadn't agreed to it. I suggested to her that those years might be better spent enjoying herself traveling.

We had a 50-50 partnership marriage. We pooled all our income and divided household chores equally. We shared all the things required to maintain a home and a relationship. I did most of the cooking and shopping for food. Kathy did most of the laundry and cleaning. We liked to garden together and split those chores. I did most of the repair work around the house like minor electrical or plumbing problems, but Kathy was the better painter and when the house needed inside painting, Kathy did that. Kathy oversaw the finances. She paid the bills each month, writing out checks on the computer. She also did the banking and the taxes. Although we talked about the investments we made, Kathy was more interested and knew more about the stock market. I followed her advice in allocating my university retirement account among different mutual funds. She was very good at that. I planned our travel. I liked to do that and had more time than Kathy in light of everything else she did plus her job, which was demanding.

I will never forget hearing about Katherine's accident, if you can call that kind of recklessness on Shrackle's part an accident. I was in my office talking to one of my students, Cheryl Tobias, when the departmental secretary knocked on the door and told me that Katherine had been in a serious accident. I rushed over to the hospital, Nita Memorial, and found her in the emergency room. She was unconscious when I first saw her. Later, in the intensive care unit, her eyes would open from time to time but she never said anything. She would moan softly during both her waking moments and even when she seemed unconscious. She appeared to be in considerable pain the whole time in the hospital.

I stayed at the hospital during the days before her death. Friends brought me clean clothes and I was able to shower there. Those were the longest four days of my life. Even when the doctors were pessimistic, I was hopeful for a miracle, but it just didn't happen. When she died, I just went back to the empty house. It took me six months before I could begin to clear out some of her clothes, books, and papers. I still haven't cleared it all out. I can't believe what has happened to me since Kathy's death. I sit at home day after day, watching television or listening to music. I can't even read a book. I seldom go out, except to teach my classes. I am sure that my teaching has suffered. Certainly, I no longer have the close working relationship with my students that I had when Kathy was alive. I'm alone all the time and I'm lonely.

Our house is located two blocks down from Greenview Avenue on the east side of the street. I assume Kathy was walking home at the time she was struck down by Mr. Shrackle. Kathy and I loved to walk through Senn Park. There were times we would walk through the park rather than walking all the way down Thorndale from Kirby just to enjoy the beauty of the park.

Exhibit 5 is a fair and accurate depiction of Katherine as she looked before the accident. The photograph was taken in our backyard about a year before her death.

Page 32

Q: You have developed a close relationship with one of your students, though, haven't you Mr. Potter, one to overcome the loneliness you spoke of earlier, am I right?

A: If you're speaking of Cheryl Tobias, that's true. She was and is a graduate student at the university, and had just completed a class with me as a teaching assistant in the fall semester of 2021 when Kathy died.

Q: Ironically, she was actually in your office when you got the news about Kathy's accident, right?

A: That's right.

Q: Let me show you Exhibit 35, which are ImageGram posts by Ms. Tobias made on a trip you two took to Martinique six months after your wife's death.

A: Where did you get these?

Q: My question, Mr. Potter, is whether the photographs shown in these five Image-Gram posts accurately show you and Ms. Tobias on the beach in Martinique, show your bedroom at the Martinique Princess Hotel, the people who went on one of the two champagne cruises you and Ms. Tobias took on that trip, and a sunset you both enjoyed while in Martinique.

A: I am not aware of any ImageGram posts made by Ms. Tobias then or since.

Q: That may well be, Mr. Potter, but I am asking you if these five photographs accurately show portions of the trip to Martinique you enjoyed with Ms. Tobias in June of 2023?

A: They appear to.

Because of our personal relationship, I have not supervised any of Ms. Tobias' work since the fall 2022 semester. That would have been improper given our relationship. Despite our age difference, she's twenty-four, we have a lot in common and Cheryl shares my interest in traveling. Yes, Exhibits 36 and 37 are travel records from our trip to Martinique and Exhibit 38 is a copy of our hotel bill from that same trip. Yes, I paid the entire cost of the trip.

Our relationship is developing slowly. We have been intimate, but Cheryl has not moved in with me, or me with her, and we have no plans to do so. I can't say what will happen in the future. Our age difference doesn't bother Cheryl, but I'm concerned it will become a problem in the future. Also, she has her whole career ahead of her. She's very bright and I don't know how that will jibe with my work plans in the future. Although I value my relationship with Cheryl and she's helped me deal with Kathy's death, she'll never take Kathy's place in my heart, and I doubt my relationship with Cheryl will ever be as fulfilling as what I had with Kathy. We were soulmates and I think that only happens once in your life if you're lucky.

Yes, I still live in the same house Kathy and I bought together.

Exhibit 26 is the bill from Nita Memorial Hospital, which has been paid. Exhibit 27 is the invoice from the funeral home, which also has been paid.

I have read the foregoing and it is a true and accurate transcription of my deposition testimony given January 18, 2023.

Signed: Date: January 18, 2023

Jeffrey T. Potter

Jeffrey Potter

Subscribed and sworn before me this 18th day of January, 2023.

Harry Gibbons

Harry Gibbons

Notary

SUMMARY OF DEPOSITION OF DANIEL SLOAN

I am forty-eight years old. I am the principal shareholder and chief executive officer of Techno-Soft, Inc. We are a small company with about fifty employees. We provide software for various high-tech manufacturing companies. The software we have developed is used in delicate manufacturing processes in the electronics industry.

Katherine Potter started working for us in 2010. Her starting salary was $34,000 a year. Her salary increased on an annual basis until, in 2021, she was making a base salary of $85,000 in the position of technology training specialist. At the time of her death, her fringe benefits package was twenty percent of her salary. This included contribution to the retirement plan, medical, and dental insurance, as well as life and disability insurance. As an example of what we thought of her, we gave her a bonus of $10,000 in January 2021. The bonus was, in part, simply a recognition of her value to the company but it was also in recognition of the fact that she had spent more than ten years with us. Through our human resources director, Linda Graham, I provided all of the details of her employment to Robert Glenn, the economist working for Mr. Potter's lawyer.

Katherine was one of our prized employees. She consistently received raises at the highest level of all employees. I fully expected her to continue that pattern. She was smart and worked very hard. She also was very ambitious. She kept talking about all those years she spent working for peanuts as a high school teacher. In fact, I was grooming her to become an executive vice president, she was that good. No, it wasn't certain that she would be made a vice president. If she did receive that promotion—and in my opinion there was a good chance she would have—it likely would have occurred in three or so years, by about 2024 or 2025. The current salary range for that position is $120,000 to $150,000 a year. Also, people at that level typically receive bonuses in the $15,000 range based on good performance. Our business is expanding, and Katherine was exactly the kind of person we needed. She had all of the technical skills as well as an extraordinary ability to work with people.

Katherine did tell me that her husband, Jeffrey, was always after her to retire early. He's a college professor and has the summers off. They both loved to travel. Katherine told me that this was Jeff's dream and she had told him that she would think about it. She told me that there was no way that she would retire before she was sixty. She told me that she loved her job and that all of the things she did with Jeff were okay, but work was really her first love. I am absolutely confident she would have stayed on.

Even in the very remote possibility that she would have left her current duties, she could have gone part-time. A number of our employees in their fifties have done that and, given the nature of our work, we can accommodate them by permitting them to work from home.

We'll sure miss Katherine. I hope that Jeffrey gets through all of this in one piece. I've always seen him as a pretty fragile guy.

I have read the foregoing and it is a true and accurate transcription of my deposition testimony given January 19, 2023.

Signed: Date: January 19, 2023

Daniel Sloan

Subscribed and sworn before me this 19th day of January, 2023.

Harry Gibbons

Notary

DEFENDANTS' DEPOSITIONS

Summary of Deposition of Charles T. Shrackle

I am Charles T. Shrackle, one of the defendants in this case. I live at 1701 West Johnston, Nita City. I am thirty-eight years old.

I am a self-employed excavating contractor. I started my business, the Shrackle Construction Company, four years ago. Before that time, I worked for various construction firms as a supervisor. Shrackle is a small business corporation. My wife Emily and I are the only stockholders. We dig trenches for dry wells, sewer or water pipes, or for electrical conduits, and install the pipes or other hardware necessary for the jobs. Then we anchor the job, usually with cement, and after the work is checked and approved, refill the excavation. The firm only does excavation work. We work for developers, for public utilities, and for state and local government. We have twelve full-time employees and hire a number of laborers each day depending on what work we are doing. We may have as many as fifteen extra people working for us on any given day. Although much of our equipment is rented to fit our needs for particular jobs, we own some, including a backhoe and a couple of dump trucks. We have an excavator and bulldozer on one-year leases. On November 30, 2021, we were involved in a couple of sewer excavation projects. One was a relatively small one for the city at the corner of John and Holiday Park at the north end of town. The other was a very large project for an extension of the Greenbriar Manor subdivision. Greenbriar Manor is on the south end of town. This project has been giving us some problems. We were past the due date for completion of our portion of the job. It wasn't our fault. We ran into some rock we hadn't expected to find but the general contractor, Clark Poe, was not particularly sympathetic. In fact, Poe had summoned me to a meeting on the afternoon of the accident. He had emailed me asking to meet with him, which was a little unusual. Exhibit 23 is that email. We were supposed to meet at the site at about 3:30. Exhibit 24 is the reply email I sent back to him.

On the morning of the accident, I got up at 6:45 a.m., my usual time. I had gotten a good night's sleep, probably about seven hours. I was taking no medication and the state of my health was good. I had not had any alcoholic beverages either on the day of the accident or on the day before. I don't use drugs of any kind.

I started the day at my office, which is in Sommers Township, just at the northeast part of town. I called my crews on my cell phone and got them organized and working, then went to the John and Holiday Park site. I stayed there most of the day. We were putting the finishing touches on a sewer we had installed. I left at about 2:30 p.m. because I had to make a stop at Nita Builders Supply, which is located near downtown—a couple of miles from the Holiday Park site. I ordered some material there and got to talking with some of the staff and other customers. One contractor was complaining about how bad business was and how much trouble he was having with some of his subcontractors. He wanted advice on how to cut their charges and how to get them to get their work done on schedule. I realized I was running a little late for my meeting with Poe at Greenbriar, so I cut the conversation short and headed for Greenbriar. I was by myself.

Greenbriar is located on South Mattis Street, about five miles from where the accident occurred. I would guess I left Builders Supply about ten after three.

Page 22

Q. What did you do once you left Builders Supply?

A. I drove down First Street heading out of town. When I got to Kirby I turned right.

Q. How long did that take?

A. It's about a half mile to Kirby, so I'd say no more than five or ten minutes.

Q. Once you turned onto Kirby, what did you do?

A. I went straight to Mattis so I could turn and head out to Greenbriar. Mattis is about ten blocks down the way.

Q. Did you use your cell phone during this time at all?

A. Yes. When I turned onto Kirby, I called Poe on my cell phone to tell him I would be a little bit late.

Q. Tell me about that conversation.

A. It was a quick call, less than a minute. Poe told me not to sweat being a little late, but he did say he had to leave for an appointment at 4:00, so I should get there as soon as I could.

Q. Were you still on the phone when you arrived at Mattis?

A. I'm not sure. I may have still been talking to him when I got there.

The intersection of Mattis and Kirby is about a mile down from where I turned onto Kirby. The light was green. There was moderate traffic. I did not come to a complete stop, but slowed for a car that went by before I could make a left turn to go south on Mattis. I started my turn from the southernmost westbound lane of Kirby. Exhibit 16 shows the left-turn lane I was in on the right side of the photograph, and the median I drove around on Mattis on the left side of the photo. Exhibit 11 shows cars making the same turn I made from Kirby onto Mattis.

I made a gradual turn to the east, southbound lane of Mattis. I saw some schoolchildren, three I think, on the southwest corner of the intersection—where Jim Marshall's car wash is. They were just standing there. I had my eye on them in case one should dart into the path of the car. I didn't know any of the kids and I don't remember much else about them. I think I also saw a crossing guard on the corner by White Castle. I don't remember any other pedestrians.

I remember making the turn and there was the impact and that was it. The impact took place several seconds after I passed south of the Kirby Avenue sidewalk. I was on the inside lane probably about four feet away from the median.

I did not see Ms. Potter before the impact. I did not apply my brakes before the impact, although as I made the turn, I had my foot on the brake pedal. I usually make my left turns that way. I was probably traveling about fifteen miles an hour at the time of the impact.

I remember that it was a clear day and that the sun was out. I had to squint as I was making the turn because Mattis at that point goes southwest and at that time of day the sun was pretty low in the sky. I could still see in front of me. I had my eye on the children on the corner all the time.

I both heard and felt the impact, but I didn't immediately know what I had hit. The impact was on the left front of my vehicle. As soon as I felt the impact, I applied the brakes with as much force as I could. As I said, my foot was already on the brake. The vehicle stopped quickly, and I jumped out. I moved around the front of the car, and I saw Ms. Potter lying under it. She was lying almost straight, with her head under the front bumper and her feet straight back. Her head was pointed south and her feet north. She seemed to be conscious, and I asked her, "Where did you come from?" She didn't reply.

The police arrived almost immediately. We got a first-aid kit out of my truck and applied a compress to her forehead, and we waited for the ambulance to come. There were skid marks and the police measured them. There was a mark on the left-hand side of the hood of my truck, near the division between the hood and the fender.

At the time of the accident, I was driving my 2007 Toyota Tacoma truck. My truck was in good condition at the time of the accident. It had been inspected and the brakes checked about a month before the accident. The tires were relatively new. I think they had less than 5,000 miles on them. Exhibit 6 shows me and my truck at a job site out in Ferndale just after I got it. Yeah, I am talking on my cell phone in that picture, it seems like half this job is solving problems and coordinating jobs on the phone. The logo shown on the truck in that exhibit, and more closely in Exhibit 8, is my company logo.

At the time of the accident, I was covered by an automobile liability policy of $500,000 per person and $1 million per accident. The policy was with Boston Casualty. The policy number is FA606560, effective September 23, 2021, to September 23, 2023. Except for the fact that there is concern that this action will exceed the policy limits, the insurance company hasn't indicated any problem with my coverage. I also have a $5 million umbrella policy for the company with Boston Casualty. They have also been notified about this accident.

I did not meet with Clark Poe at Greenbriar that day. Shortly after they took Ms. Potter away in the ambulance, I texted him saying what happened and why I didn't get there as promised. (Exhibit 32 is that text.) We met the next day. Based on our conversation, there was a reduction in the amount we were to be paid for the job. I wasn't too happy about the result, but compared to Ms. Potter's situation it was no big deal.

Ordinarily it would take me about twenty minutes to get from Builders Supply to Greenbrier. However, it could take longer on weekday afternoons about that time because of the schools getting out. The traffic was a little heavy before I got to the intersection of Kirby and Mattis, but not too bad. I thought that it might get worse after I turned on Mattis, particularly down about a mile when the road narrows. It's highway at that point, but two lanes. But I felt I'd make it in plenty of time for my meeting with Poe.

I have read the foregoing and it is a true and accurate transcription of my deposition testimony given on February 16, 2023.

Signed: Date: February 16, 2023

Charles T. Shrackle

Charles T. Shrackle

Subscribed and sworn before me this 16th day of February, 2023.

Terry Anderson

Terry Anderson

Notary

SUMMARY OF DEPOSITION OF ALICE MALLORY

My name is Alice Mallory. I am forty-seven years old. I am married and have two children, both of whom are in high school. I work part-time as a school crossing guard at the corner of Mattis and Kirby. I have done that work for about two years. I work both in the morning and in the afternoon at that corner.

On the afternoon of November 30, 2021, I was working on the southwest corner of the inter-section. At about 3:25, I crossed over to the southeast corner of the street by the White Castle to reprimand a small boy who had not heeded my warning to stop. He had run out in front of some cars but luckily wasn't hurt. I was extremely upset by the incident. The boy could have been killed. It would be the worst thing I could imagine a child being killed while I was the guard. Exhibit 9 shows where I started out in the foreground, and also where I was in front of the White Castle when I saw Ms. Potter across the street. As I knelt to talk to him, I saw a woman in my peripheral vision; I later learned this was Ms. Katherine Potter. She crossed the street from west to east in the crosswalk. I can't remember what she was wearing or much about her, but I remember that she had dark hair.

When she reached the median, she suddenly turned south and began to walk south on the median strip. I looked down to continue talking to the boy, then heard a thump and looked up instantly. I saw Ms. Potter being carried on the hood of a pickup truck about thirty feet south of the crosswalk. The truck stopped about twenty feet later. I ran over to see if I could help, but others got there before me, so I returned to looking after the children.

At the time I was watching Ms. Potter, I was also watching children on the other corner. I was really concerned that one of them would cross the street in a dangerous way. However, I did clearly see all that I have said here. I did not come forward as a witness originally because I was upset and didn't want my story to hurt Ms. Potter or her family. I was finally contacted by the defendant's lawyer and told her what I saw.

Three weeks after this incident, just before Christmas, I resigned my position as a school cross-ing guard. The tension of looking after children was too much for me. I guess I was also affected by Ms. Potter's accident and death.

Also, my eyesight has become worse. I have a degenerative eye condition that will get pro-gressively worse as I age. I still see pretty well with corrective lenses and feel that I could have kept on as a guard for a little longer. However, the pressure of concern for the children and the trauma of the accident caused me to quit early.

Yes, I was wearing my corrective lenses at the time of the accident. My sight is normal with those lenses although there are some limits to my peripheral vision. I have what is known as primary open-angle glaucoma. It was undiagnosed for a long time and hadn't been diagnosed at the time of the accident. They discovered that my central vision is fine, but that I have some weakening peripheral vision. It was just starting to be a problem at the time of the accident. I had surgery about two months ago that my doctor says will correct most of the problem.

I have read the foregoing and it is a true and accurate transcription of my deposition testimony given on February 13, 2023.

Signed: Date: February 13, 2023

Alice Mallory

Signed and sworn to before me this 13th day of February, 2023.

Able Ames

Notary

SUMMARY OF DEPOSITION OF JUANITA WILLIAMS

My name is Juanita Williams. I live at 1010 West Kirby, Unit 15, in Nita City. I work part-time as a secretary. I am a single mother with two children, Victoria, age ten, and Joshua, age three.

On November 30, 2021, at approximately 3:30 p.m., I was at the corner of Kirby and Mattis. I was stopped on Kirby Avenue, west of the intersection, facing east getting ready for the light to change to green. I had just picked up Victoria at Senn School and was driving my green 2019 Toyota Highlander to pick up Josh at his day care.

A man in a pickup truck was in the left-hand lane of westbound Kirby on the opposite side of the intersection with his left turn signal on as he was waiting to turn southwest on Mattis. It looked like he was talking on his cell phone, or he may have simply had his hand up to his ear. The light changed to green, he waited until I had passed, and with the light still green he turned southwest on Mattis. The pickup truck took the turn a little fast, maybe at about twenty miles an hour. He sort of rolled through the intersection and then picked up speed.

I actually didn't see him hit the dark-haired woman, who I later found out was Ms. Potter, but he could not have been going fast because I was only a few feet from the intersection when my daughter screamed, "Mom, someone was just hit." We immediately turned around and went back to the accident.

When we went back to the intersection and parked at the White Castle, I saw the dark-haired woman lying underneath the pickup truck. I saw that funny Superman logo on the truck.

I didn't know Ms. Potter or anyone in her family. I don't know Charles Shrackle and I never heard of Shrackle Construction Company until the time of the accident.

I have read the foregoing and it is a true and accurate transcription of my deposition testimony given on February 13, 2023.

Signed: Date: February 13, 2023

Juanita Williams
Signed and sworn to before me this 13th day of February, 2023.

Joseph Lucey
Notary

Summary of Deposition of Victoria Williams

My name is Vicky Williams, and I am ten years old. I live at 1010 W. Kirby Avenue in Nita City with my mom and my brother, Joshua. Joshua is three.

My mom was driving me home from school on November 30, 2021. She always picks me up. I was in the back seat in the car on the passenger side. I don't remember if I had my seat belt on, but I usually do. I think it was about 3:30 in the afternoon when the accident happened.

We were headed toward town on Kirby Avenue. On the map you showed me that would be going east. (Exhibit 3) We stopped for a light where Kirby crosses Mattis near the White Castle. There was a man in a truck coming towards us on the opposite side of the intersection getting ready to make a left turn onto Mattis. I was looking out the side window at some of my school friends who were on the sidewalk in front of the car wash. There were three or four of them. I waved and smiled at my friends trying to get their attention.

Mom started driving across the intersection. I twisted around to look out the back window and saw the man in the truck turn after we passed him. I saw him because I was looking towards my friends. A lady with black or brown hair, I think, was standing on the center strip on Mattis a little down from the crosswalk. She was facing towards my friends with her back to us. She just stepped right off the center strip right in front of the truck. I saw the truck hit her and her purse went flying into the air. The truck screeched his brakes and stopped. You're right that the sun was a little in my eyes, but I could see what happened to the lady. I probably just put my hand up to my forehead so I could see my friends even though the sun was out, but I really don't remember. I know I could see what I told you about.

I yelled to my mom about what just happened, that the truck hit someone. She turned around and we went back and parked in the White Castle parking lot. I saw the lady that got hit lying underneath the truck. It was pretty scary.

Page 14

Q. Where was the woman when you first saw her?

A. She was down the crosswalk on Mattis.

Q. Do you mean south of the crosswalk?

A. I'm not too good with directions. She was away from Kirby Street.

Q. How many feet was she away from Kirby?

A. I'm not too good with guessing feet. I would say maybe twenty feet.

Q. Could it have been less?

A. Maybe, but I'd say about twenty. Fifteen or twenty.

Q. How wide is Mattis Avenue at that point?

A. Gee, I don't know. Probably a couple of hundred feet wide.

I looked at the map and picture that you called Exhibit 17, and it shows about where we were and what I could see when I first saw the lady standing on the center strip. The map and picture that you called Exhibit 18 shows about where we were when I saw the purse flying in the air.

I have read the foregoing and it is a true and accurate transcription of my deposition testimony given on February 13, 2023.

Signed: Date: February 13, 2023

Victoria Williams

Victoria Williams

Signed and sworn to before me this 13th day of February, 2023.

Joseph Lucey

Joseph Lucey
Notary

Summary of Deposition of Benjamin Grimson

My name is Benjamin Grimson. I just turned nineteen years old. I am presently in prison at Allenwood Prison in Allenwood, Nita.

On November 30 last year, I was cruising down Mattis in a Camry when I stopped for a burger and fries at the White Castle on Kirby. My buddy, Eddie, works there and he waited on me at the drive-through after I placed my order. As I was heading away from the drive-through window, I heard a loud thump and when I looked over there was this lady flying in the air on the front of a truck. I yelled, "Holy shit, somebody smashed up that lady." When I saw her, she was in mid-air. At that point, I'd say she was about ten feet south of the crosswalk. The truck must have carried her another thirty-five feet or so. When I saw the truck carrying her, it looked like it was still going pretty fast, maybe twenty miles an hour. The truck stopped and the driver got out of the truck. He said something but I couldn't hear what it was. A bunch of people ran over to her. I decided there wasn't anything I could do. There wasn't anybody behind me, so I backed up and went out the Kirby Street entrance.

I drove a couple of blocks east on Kirby and pulled into a parking space on the street. I ate my hamburger and texted Eddie. (Exhibit 32 is that text.)

The picture that says Exhibit 19 shows the drive-through lane at the White Castle. Exhibit 20 shows what you can see of Mattis Avenue from further down the drive-through lane. That's where I was when I saw this lady.

Eddie must have told somebody I had been at the drive-through window when the accident occurred. He also told you where to find me.

On February 25, 2023, I was arrested for grand larceny automobile. I was charged as an adult with the theft of several cars, including the 2019 Toyota Camry I was driving when I saw the accident. The car belonged to one of the teachers at my high school. I am now serving a sentence of two years at Allenwood, which is a minimum-security Nita prison.

I have read the foregoing and it is a true and accurate transcription of my deposition testimony given on February 17, 2023.

Signed: Date: February 17, 2023

Benjamin Grimson

Benjamin Grimson
Subscribed and sworn to before me this 17th day of February, 2023.

Tracy Williams

Tracy Williams
Notary

Expert Reports

Expert Report of Robert Glenn, PhD

Professor of Economics

University of Nita

State of Nita Circuit Court
Circuit Court of Darrow
County Civil Division

Jeffrey T. Potter, the Administrator of the Estate of Katherine Potter,
and Jeffrey T. Potter, individually
(Plaintiff)

v.

Charles T. Shrackle and The Shrackle Construction Company
(Defendants)

Dated: February 1, 2023

Introduction

I, Robert Glenn, understand this matter involves Jeffrey T. Potter, the Administrator of the Estate of Katherine Potter, and Jeffrey T. Potter, individually, as plaintiff, and Charles T. Shrackle and The Shrackle Construction Company (collectively, "Shrackle") as defendants. As I understand this matter, Ms. Katherine Potter was struck by an automobile driven by Mr. Charles T. Shrackle on November 30, 2021. Ms. Potter died on December 4, 2021, as a result of injuries sustained in that accident.

Engagement of Robert Glenn

As part of this engagement, Madden & James, counsel for plaintiffs, requested that I:

1. Review the Potter v. Shrackle case file, including but not limited to:

   a. the complaint and answer;

   b. statements of Marilyn J. Kelly, Juanita Williams, Victoria Williams, Alice Mallory, and Benjamin Grimson;

   c. depositions of James Marshall, Victoria Williams, Michael Young, Charles T. Shrackle, Jeffrey Potter, and Daniel Sloan; and

   d. other documents provided by counsel;

2. Collect information relevant to a calculation of economic losses resulting from a wrongful death; and

3. Provide economic and statistical analysis regarding plaintiff's specific claims.

In preparing my analysis, I have relied on counsel, Madden & James, for any interpretation of legal issues.

Supplemental Analysis and Opinions

I understand that discovery in this matter is still ongoing and that additional documents, statements, depositions, or trial testimony on topics relevant to the opinions issued in this report may be forthcoming. As a result, I reserve the right to supplement this report or to address any such testimony at trial.

Opinion

Based upon my continuing review and analysis of the Potter v. Shrackle case file, supplemented with my own research of relevant economic and demographic information, I have developed the following opinion regarding economic damages in this matter.

1. From the date of her death through her eventual retirement at age 60, the value of Katherine Potter's lost earnings, benefits and household work, and net of her consumption is a loss of $2,334,579 to her estate and to her husband, Jeffrey Potter. In present discounted value, this amount is a loss of $1,532,021 to the plaintiff.

Bases for Opinions

1. Katherine Potter was in good health at the time of her death and would have reasonably been expected to work until at least the age of 60 before her retirement.

2. Katherine Potter was happy with her position as a Technology Training Specialist at Techno-Soft, Inc. I believe the pattern of her salary growth from the date of her death to her eventual retirement at age 60 would be similar to the average pattern of salary growth during her period of employment with the company.

3. Katherine Potter would have continued to enjoy her fringe benefits as an employee of Techno-Soft, Inc. I have spoken with Ms. Linda Graham, human resources director at Techno-Soft, Inc. and have learned that Katherine Potter's benefits amounted to 20 percent of her income at the time of her death.

4. Katherine Potter shared equally in the household work with her husband, Jeffrey Potter, and her death will result in a loss equal to the value of Katherine's labor, which equaled approximately $41 per hour at the date of her death.

Exhibits

For purposes of presenting our opinions and their bases, I may develop and use exhibits including overheads, flip charts, and other summary graphics. I may also use certain demonstrative aids and illustrations in presenting technical concepts and analyses.

Compensation

The hourly rates for myself and my research associates who worked on this matter range between $75 and $350 per hour. My hourly rate is $350 per hour.

Qualifications

I am a professor of economics at the University of Nita in Nita City with fields of concentration in labor economics and microeconomics. I hold a bachelor's degree in economics from the University of North Carolina (2004) and a PhD in economics from the University of Illinois (2008). I have taught economics at the undergraduate and graduate level at the University of Nita for fourteen years as well as numerous seminars in the industry. As part of my duties as a professor at a research institution, I direct graduate research, conduct independent research, and publish my results in academic economic journals. In addition to my publications, I have received research grants from the National Science Foundation, the Social Science Research Council, the Center for Comparative Studies at the University of Nita, and the Nita Law Enforcement Commission.

February 1, 2023

Robert Glenn

Professor of Economics, University of Nita

**POTTER V. SHRACKLE AND THE SHRACKLE CONSTRUCTION COMPANY
DAMAGES MODEL OF ROBERT GLENN, PhD**

TABLE 1. SUMMARY OF ECONOMIC LOSS, WRONGFUL DEATH OF KATHERINE POTTER

Summary of Economic Loss

		Nominal Dollars	*Present Discounted Value*
A.	Future Value of Earnings	$2,918,363	$1,915,118
B.	Future Value of Fringe Benefits	$583,673	$383,024
C.	Future Value of Household Work	$1,024,233	$672,133
D.	Future Value of Personal Consumption	$2,191,691	$1,438,254
E.	Total Value of Loss (A + B + C - D)	$2,334,579	$1,532,021

**POTTER V. SHRACKLE AND THE SHRACKLE CONSTRUCTION COMPANY
DAMAGES MODEL OF ROBERT GLENN, PhD**

TABLE 2. FUTURE VALUE OF EARNINGS OF KATHERINE POTTER AGE 45 TO 60

Date of Birth:	June 15, 1976
Date of Death:	December 4, 2021
Appraisal Period:	2023 to 2036
Projected Retirement Age:	60
Discount Rate:	6.00%
Earnings Growth Rate:	9.80%

Year	Projected Age	Projected Value Earnings	Present Discounted Value of Earnings
2021	45	$85,000	
2022	46	$93,329	$93,329
2023	47	$102,474	$102,474
2024	48	$112,515	$106,146
2025	49	$123,540	$109,950
2026	50	$135,645	$113,890
2027	51	$148,936	$117,971
2028	52	$163,530	$122,199
2029	53	$179,554	$126,578
2030	54	$197,147	$131,114
2031	55	$216,465	$135,813
2032	56	$237,676	$140,680
2033	57	$260,965	$145,721
2034	58	$286,536	$150,943
2035	59	$314,612	$156,353
2036	60	$345,440	$161,956
	Value of Future Earnings:	$2,918,363	$1,915,118

POTTER V. SHRACKLE AND THE SHRACKLE CONSTRUCTION COMPANY
DAMAGES MODEL OF ROBERT GLENN, PhD

TABLE 3. HISTORICAL EARNINGS GROWTH OF KATHERINE POTTER, 1997 TO 2021

Date of Birth: June 15, 1976
Date of Death: December 4, 2021
Observation Period: 1997 to 2021

Year	Age	Earnings	% Change from Previous Year	Job
1998 to 2000	22-24	$0	n/a	(1)
2001	25	$19,000	n/a	(2)
2002	26	$19,600	3.2%	(2)
2003	27	$20,250	3.3%	(2)
2004	28	$20,900	3.2%	(2)
2005	29	$21,600	3.3%	(2)
2006	30	$22,300	3.2%	(2)
2007	31	$23,000	3.1%	(2)
2008	32	$23,750	3.3%	(2)
2009	33	$24,500	3.2%	(2)
2010	34	$25,400	3.7%	(2)/(3)
2011	35	$34,000	33.9%	(3)
2012	36	$42,000	23.5%	(3)
2013	37	$50,000	19.0%	(3)
2014	38	$57,500	15.0%	(3)
2015	39	$62,500	8.7%	(3)
2016	40	$67,500	8.0%	(3)
2017	41	$71,000	5.2%	(3)
2018	42	$73,500	3.5%	(3)
2019	43	$76,000	3.4%	(3)
2020	44	$78,000	2.6%	(3)
2021	45	$85,000	9.0%	(3)
2022	Deceased	$0	100.0%	Deceased
Average Income Growth Rate (2010 to 2020): 9.80%				

Job Information:

(1)   Attending Graduate School, University of Nita

(2)   Computer Instructor, Nita City Unified School District

(3)   Computer Instructor, Techno-Soft, Inc.

POTTER V. SHRACKLE AND THE SHRACKLE CONSTRUCTION COMPANY
DAMAGES MODEL OF ROBERT GLENN, PhD

TABLE 4. FUTURE VALUE OF FRINGE BENEFITS OF KATHERINE POTTER, AGE 45 TO 60

Date of Birth:	June 15, 1976
Date of Death:	December 4, 2021
Appraisal Period:	2021 to 2036
Projected Retirement Age:	60
Discount Rate:	6.00%
Benefits as % of Income:	20%

Year	Projected Age	Projected Value of Fringe Benefits	Present Discounted Value of Fringe Benefits
2021	45	$17,000	
2022	46	$18,666	$18,666
2023	47	$20,495	$20,495
2024	48	$22,503	$21,229
2025	49	$24,708	$21,990
2026	50	$27,129	$22,778
2027	51	$29,787	$23,594
2028	52	$32,706	$24,440
2029	53	$35,911	$25,316
2030	54	$39,429	$26,223
2031	55	$43,293	$27,163
2032	56	$47,535	$28,136
2033	57	$52,193	$29,144
2034	58	$57,307	$30,189
2035	59	$62,922	$31,271
2036	60	$69,088	$32,391
Value of Future Fringe Benefits:		$583,673	$383,024

POTTER V. SHRACKLE AND THE SHRACKLE CONSTRUCTION COMPANY
DAMAGES MODEL OF ROBERT GLENN, PhD

TABLE 5. FUTURE VALUE OF HOUSEHOLD WORK OF KATHERINE POTTER, AGE 45 TO 60

Date of Birth:	June 15, 1976
Date of Death:	December 4, 2021
Appraisal Period:	2023 to 2036
Projected Retirement Age:	60
Discount Rate:	6.00%
# of Hours Per Day at Household Work:	2
Days Per Year Doing Household Work:	365

Year	Projected Age	Projected Value of Household Work	Present Discounted Value of Household Work
2021	45	$29,832	
2022	46	$32,755	$32,755
2023	47	$35,964	$35,964
2024	48	$39,488	$37,253
2025	49	$43,358	$38,588
2026	50	$47,606	$39,971
2027	51	$52,271	$41,403
2028	52	$57,393	$42,887
2029	53	$63,016	$44,424
2030	54	$69,191	$46,016
2031	55	$75,971	$47,665
2032	56	$83,415	$49,373
2032	57	$91,589	$51,143
2034	58	$100,563	$52,975
2035	59	$110,417	$54,874
2036	60	$121,236	$56,840
Value of Future Household Work:		$1,024,233	$672,133

Assumption:

(1)   There are 2,080 work hours in a year (52 weeks * 40 hours per week).

POTTER V. SHRACKLE AND THE SHRACKLE CONSTRUCTION COMPANY
DAMAGES MODEL OF ROBERT GLENN, PhD

TABLE 6. FUTURE VALUE OF PERSONAL CONSUMPTION OF KATHERINE POTTER, AGE 45 TO 60

Date of Birth:	June 15, 1976
Date of Death:	December 4, 2021
Appraisal Period:	2023 to 2036
Projected Retirement Age:	60
Discount Rate:	6.00%
Consumption as % of Income:	75.10%

Year	Projected Age	Projected Value of Personal Consumption	Present Discounted Value of Personal Consumption
2021	45	$63,835	
2022	46	$70,090	$70,090
2023	47	$76,958	$76,958
2024	48	$84,499	$79,716
2025	49	$92,778	$82,572
2026	50	$101,869	$85,531
2027	51	$111,851	$88,597
2028	52	$122,811	$91,772
2029	53	$134,845	$95,060
2030	54	$148,058	$98,467
2031	55	$162,565	$101,996
2032	56	$178,495	$105,651
2033	57	$195,985	$109,437
2034	58	$215,188	$113,359
2035	59	$236,274	$117,421
2036	60	$259,425	$121,629
Value of Future Consumption:		$2,191,691	$1,438,254

POTTER V. SHRACKLE AND THE SHRACKLE CONSTRUCTION COMPANY
DAMAGES MODEL OF ROBERT GLENN, PhD

TABLE 6. FUTURE VALUE OF PERSONAL CONSUMPTION OF KATHERINE POTTER,
AGE 45 TO 60

TABLE 6 NOTES

(1) To arrive at Katherine Potter's net contribution to the Potter household welfare (i.e., what Jeffrey Potter will lose monetarily as a result of his wife's death), the future value of Katherine's consumption expenditures should be subtracted from the future value of her income, fringe benefits, and household work.

(2) The U.S. Department of Labor has calculated that, on average, household expenditures amount to 89.1 percent of household income for American households.

(3) Of this amount, on average, 28 percent of household income is spent on housing expenses.

(4) In this matter, half of this amount should be excluded from Katherine Potter's share of income spent on household expenses since housing is a benefit equally shared by both Katherine and Jeffrey Potter. Katherine's death is a loss to Mr. Potter insofar as Katherine contributed to the cost of housing for their household.

(5) As a result, 75.1 percent of Katherine's future wage and salary earnings should be subtracted from her total wage and salary earnings to account for the value of her expenditures.

Source: State of NITA Department of Labor, Consumer Expenditures in 2021, May 2023.

Robert Glenn, PhD
Goldman Sachs Professor of Economics
University of Nita, Department of Economics, Campus Locator #43
Nita City, Nita
(555) 444-2308, Fax (555) 444-2307
glennecon@email.nita.edu

Education

BS University of North Carolina (2002) (economics)

PhD University of Illinois (2007) (economics)

Employment History

Assistant Professor, University of Nita, 2007–2013

Associate Professor, University of Nita, 2013–2017

Professor, University of Nita, 2017–2023

Goldman Sachs Professor, 2023–

Principal Publications since 2011:

Books

Microeconomics in a Time of Terrorism, Oxford University Press (2023)
Loss Evaluation in Wrongful Death Cases, Aspen (2019)

Articles

"The Effect of September 11 on Microeconomic Theory," 80 *Harvard Public Policy Review* 1769 (2023)

"Is Your Loss Worth Anything?" 5 *Journal of Law and Economics* 1289 (2019)

"Can Our Economic System Survive a Terrorist Attack? " 45 *Economics and Politics* 549 (2018)

"Valuing Services and Potential Retirement, "19 *Journal of Labor Economics* 42 (2014)

Sample Expert Testimony

(I have been qualified as an expert in economics in 24 different cases. I have testified for the plaintiff in all but three cases.)

Michaels v. Hammer, North Carolina Superior Court, October 2023 (personal injury, testified for plaintiff)

Smith v. Tucker, United States District Court (SDNY) (personal injury, testified for plaintiff)

Rosen v. Nichol, United States District Court (S. D. Calif.) (wrongful death, testified for plaintiff)

Glandon v. Schwartz, Nita Superior Court, May 2018 (wrongful death case, testified for plaintiff)

State of Nita Circuit Court Circuit Court of Darrow
County Civil Division

Jeffrey T. Potter, the Administrator of the Estate
of Katherine Potter, and Jeffrey T. Potter,
individually
(Plaintiff)

v.

Charles T. Shrackle and
The Shrackle Construction Company
(Defendants)

Expert Report of Elizabeth Buchanan, PhD
Assistant Professor of Economics, Nita State University
Nita City, Nita

March 2, 2023

1.0   Introduction

I, Elizabeth C. Buchanan, PhD, understand this matter involves Jeffrey T. Potter, the Administrator of the Estate of Katherine Potter, and Jeffrey T. Potter, individually, as plaintiff, and Charles T. Shrackle and The Shrackle Construction Company (collectively, Shrackle) as defendants. As I understand this matter, Ms. Katherine Potter was struck by an automobile driven by Mr. Charles T. Shrackle on November 30, 2021. Ms. Potter died on December 4, 2021, as a result of injuries sustained in that accident.

2.0   Qualifications

I am an assistant professor of economics at Nita State University with fields of concentration in labor economics and industrial organization. I am also a graduate of the University of Nita, holding both a bachelors and doctorate degree in economics. I have taught at Nita State University for the past five years: two years as a visiting professor, two years as a lecturer, and one year as an assistant professor. Appendix A is a copy of my current resume. It contains a listing of my papers and publications for the past ten years.

2.1   Engagement of Elizabeth Buchanan

As part of this engagement, James Barber of Pierce, Johnson & Clark (Pierce), counsel for defendants Shrackle, requested that I:

- Review the expert report on damages prepared by Dr. Robert Glenn;
- Review the Potter v. Shrackle case file, including but not limited to:
  - the complaint and answer;
  - depositions of James Marshall, Victoria Williams, Michael Young, Charles T. Shrackle, Jeffrey T. Potter, and Daniel Sloan;
  - statements of Marilyn J. Kelly, Juanita Williams, Victoria Williams, Alice Mallory, Benjamin Grimson; and
  - other documents which I have reviewed which have been produced in this matter;
- Collect information relevant to a calculation of economic losses resulting from a wrongful death; and
- Provide economic and statistical analysis regarding plaintiff's specific claims.

In preparing my analysis, I have relied on counsel, Pierce, for any interpretation of legal issues.

2.2   Supplemental Analysis and Opinions

I understand that discovery in this matter is still ongoing and that additional documents, statements, deposition, or trial testimony on topics relevant to the opinions issued in this report may be forthcoming. As a result, I reserve the right to supplement this report or to address any such testimony at trial.

3.0   Opinion

Based upon my continuing review and analysis of Dr. Glenn's expert report and the Potter v. Shrackle case file, supplemented with my own research of relevant economic and demographic information, I have developed the following opinion regarding economic damages in this matter.

- Dr. Robert Glenn substantially overstates the total value of loss allegedly suffered by the plaintiff due to incorrect and inappropriate assumptions used in his damages model.

- In my own opinion, from the date of her death through her eventual retirement at age fifty-five, the value of Katherine Potter's lost earnings, benefits and household work, net of her consumption is a loss of $411,077 to her estate and to her husband, Jeffrey Potter. In present discounted value, this amount is a loss of $333,719 to the plaintiff.

4.0   Bases for Opinions

- It is my opinion that Katherine Potter would have reasonably been expected to work full-time until the age of fifty and then would work part-time until her retirement at age fifty-five. Deposition testimony from her husband, Jeffrey Potter, stated that he and Ms. Potter talked about taking an early retirement. My calculations-of-loss valuation is conservative in that it treats Ms. Potter as having worked to the age of fifty-five, which would tend to overstate the loss if she were to retire before that age.

- It is my opinion that Katherine Potter would have an average annual salary increase of 5 percent per year. Dr. Glenn averages Ms. Potter's salary increases during her entire period of employment at Techno-Soft, Inc. This method would overstate the salary increases Ms. Potter would likely receive in the period after her death. I note that her salary increases are smaller and smaller, in percentage terms, and thus the use of long-run averages would be ignorant of this trend. Instead, I use an average of her annual salary increases over the last three years to capture the fact that she may be reaching the upper salary limit of her position.

- Assume that the imputed value of benefits enjoyed by Katherine Potter is 17.5 percent of her annual salary. Like Dr. Glenn, I have spoken to Linda Graham, human resources director at Techno-Soft, Inc. Based upon my discussion with Ms. Graham, I learned that Dr. Glenn's calculation of future fringe benefits overstates this value since it ignores the fact that Katherine Potter received a special one-time bonus payout of $10,000 in 2021 for staying beyond ten years at Techno-Soft, Inc. Were this one-time payout to be removed, the actual rate of benefits would be lowered from 20 percent to 17.5 percent of her annual salary. Dr. Glenn thus overstates all future projections for fringe benefit calculations since he does not appropriately evaluate the baseline year. I use the more justifiable number of 17.5 percent in my projections.

- Although Katherine Potter shared equally in the household work with her husband, Jeffrey Potter, and her death will result in a loss equal to the value of Ms. Potter's labor, I disagree with Dr. Glenn's methodology of using her imputed hourly wage as the appropriate replacement wage. Ms. Potter's hourly wage, assuming a 2,080-hour work year, is imputed to be approximately $41 per hour. Dr. Glenn uses this amount as the value of Ms. Potter's lost labor. This methodology is incorrect in that Dr. Glenn should value the loss of Ms. Potter's household labor at its replacement cost. Since many of the household tasks did not require the use of Ms. Potter's specialized skills, I use a more appropriate measure of replacement cost, the minimum wage.

- It is my opinion that, as a member of the Potter household, Katherine Potter consumed approximately 75 percent of her annual income as her personal consumption. The amount of consumption that Ms. Potter consumed for her benefit out of her income should not be included in an award of damages to Mr. Potter as he did not necessarily benefit from this consumption during Ms. Potter's lifetime. Although Ms. Potter would continue to consume as a member of the household after her retirement, in order to be conservative in the estimate of damages, I exclude this amount from the calculation of loss to Mr. Potter. Inclusion of this stream of consumption of retirement would make the damages amount even smaller as Ms. Potter would continue to consume but not be earning any wage or salary income.

In sum, these inappropriate and inaccurate assumptions used by Dr. Glenn in his model result in a significant overstatement of any likely damages suffered. I believe that he may have overstated damages by as much as a factor of four. I believe that damages suffered by the plaintiff would not have exceeded $334,000.

5.0 Exhibits

For purposes of presenting our opinions and their bases, I may develop and use exhibits including overheads, flip charts, and other summary graphics. I may also use certain demonstrative aids and illustrations in presenting technical concepts and analyses.

6.0 Compensation

The hourly rates for myself and my research associates who worked on this matter range between $50 and $250 per hour. My hourly rate is $250 per hour.

Elizabeth C. Buchanan
Assistant Professor of Economics
Nita State University
Nita City, Nita
March 2, 2023

**POTTER V. SHRACKLE AND THE SHRACKLE CONSTRUCTION COMPANY
REBUTTAL DAMAGES MODEL OF ELIZABETH C. BUCHANAN, PhD**

TABLE 1. SUMMARY OF ECONOMIC LOSS, WRONGFUL DEATH OF KATHERINE POTTER

Summary of Economic Loss

		Nominal Dollars	*Present Discounted Value*
A.	Future Value of Earnings	$807,964	$680,250
B.	Future Value of Fringe Benefits	$141,394	$119,044
C.	Future Value of Household Work	$68,500	$45,293
D.	Future Value of Personal Consumption	$606,781	$510,868
E.	Total Value of Loss (A + B + C - D)	$411,077	$333,719

POTTER V. SHRACKLE AND THE SHRACKLE CONSTRUCTION COMPANY
REBUTTAL DAMAGES MODEL OF ELIZABETH C. BUCHANAN, PhD

TABLE 2. FUTURE VALUE OF EARNINGS OF KATHERINE POTTER, AGE 45 TO 60

Date of Birth:	June 15, 1976
Date of Death:	December 4, 2021
Appraisal Period:	2023 to 2036
Projected Retirement Age:	55
Discount Rate:	6.00%
Earnings Growth Rate:	5.00%

Year	Projected Age	% of Full-Time	Projected Value of Earnings	Present Discounted Value of Earnings
2021	45	100%	$85,000	
2022	46	100%	$89,252	$89,252
2023	47	100%	$93,717	$93,717
2024	48	100%	$98,405	$92,835
2025	49	100%	$103,328	$91,961
202	50	100%	$108,497	$91,096
2027	51	50%	$56,962	$45,119
2028	52	50%	$59,811	$44,695
2029	53	50%	$62,803	$44,274
2030	54	50%	$65,945	$43,857
2031	55	50%	$69,244	$43,445
2032	56	0%	(RETIRED)	(RETIRED)
2033	57	0%	(RETIRED)	(RETIRED)
2034	58	0%	(RETIRED)	(RETIRED)
2035	59	0%	(RETIRED)	(RETIRED)
2036	60	0%	(RETIRED)	(RETIRED)
Value of Future Earnings:			$807,964	$680,250

POTTER V. SHRACKLE AND THE SHRACKLE CONSTRUCTION COMPANY
REBUTTAL DAMAGES MODEL OF ELIZABETH C. BUCHANAN, PhD

TABLE 3. HISTORICAL EARNINGS GROWTH OF KATHERINE POTTER, 1997 TO 2021

Date of Birth:	June 15, 1976
Date of Death:	December 4, 2021
Observation Period:	1997 to 2021

Year	Age	Earnings	% Change from Previous Year	Job
1998 to 2000	22–24	$0	n/a	(1)
2001	25	$19,000	n/a	(2)
2002	26	$19,600	3.2%	(2)
2003	27	$20,250	3.3%	(2)
2004	28	$20,900	3.2%	(2)
2005	29	$21,600	3.3%	(2)
2006	30	$22,300	3.2%	(2)
2007	31	$23,000	3.1%	(2)
2008	32	$23,750	3.3%	(2)
2009	33	$24,500	3.2%	(2)
2010	34	$25,400	3.7%	(2)/(3)
2011	35	$34,000	33.9%	(3)
2012	36	$42,000	23.5%	(3)
2013	37	$50,000	19.0%	(3)
2014	38	$57,500	15.0%	(3)
2015	39	$62,500	8.7%	(3)
2016	40	$67,500	8.0%	(3)
2017	41	$71,000	5.2%	(3)
2018	42	$73,500	3.5%	(3)
2019	43	$76,000	3.4%	(3)
2020	44	$78,000	2.6%	(3)
2021	45	$85,000	9.0%	(3)
2022	Deceased	$0	−100.0%	Deceased
Average Income Growth Rate (2018 to 2020): 5.00				

Job Information:

(1) Attending Graduate School, University of Nita

(2) Computer Instructor, Nita City Unified School District

(3) Computer Instructor, Techno-Soft, Inc.

POTTER V. SHRACKLE AND THE SHRACKLE CONSTRUCTION COMPANY REBUTTAL DAMAGES MODEL OF ELIZABETH C. BUCHANAN, PhD

TABLE 4. FUTURE VALUE OF FRINGE BENEFITS OF KATHERINE POTTER, AGE 45 TO 60

Date of Birth: June 15, 1976
Date of Death: December 4, 2021
Appraisal Period: 2023 to 2036
Projected Retirement Age: 55
Discount Rate: 6.00%
Benefits as % of Income: 17.50%
Days Per Year Doing Household Work: 365

Year	Projected Age	Projected Value of Fringe Benefits	Present Discounted Value of Fringe Benefits
2021	45	$14,875	
2022	46	$15,619	$15,619
2023	47	$16,400	$16,400
2024	48	$17,221	$16,246
2025	49	$18,082	$16,093
2026	50	$18,987	$15,942
2027	51	$9,968	$7,896
2028	52	$10,467	$7,822
2029	53	$10,991	$7,748
2030	54	$11,540	$7,675
2031	55	$12,118	$7,603
2032	56	(RETIRED)	(RETIRED)
2033	51	(RETIRED)	(RETIRED)
2034	58	(RETIRED)	(RETIRED)
2035	59	(RETIRED)	(RETIRED)
2036	60	(RETIRED)	(RETIRED)
Value of Future Fringe Benefits:		$141,394	$119,044

POTTER V. SHRACKLE AND THE SHRACKLE CONSTRUCTION COMPANY
REBUTTAL DAMAGES MODEL OF ELIZABETH C. BUCHANAN, PhD

TABLE 5. FUTURE VALUE OF HOUSEHOLD WORK OF KATHERINE POTTER, AGE 45 TO 60

Date of Birth:	June 15, 1976	
Date of Death:	December 4, 2021	
Appraisal Period:	2023 to 2036	
Projected Retirement Age:	55	
Discount Rate:	6.00%	

	Before Retirement	During Retirement
# of Hours Per Day at Household Work:	2	4
Days Per Year Doing Household Work:	250	250
Total Hours Per Year:	500	1,000

Year	Projected Age	Hourly Replacement Wage for Household Work	Projected Value of Household Work	Present Discounted Value of Household Work	
2021	45	$6.00	$3,000		
2022	46	$6.00	$3,000	$3,000	
2023	47	$6.00	$3,000	$3,000	
2024	48	$6.00	$3,000	$2,830	
2025	49	$6.00	$3,000	$2,670	
2026	50	$6.50	$3,250	$2,729	
2027	51	$6.50	$3,250	$2,574	
2028	52	$6.50	$3,250	$2,429	
2029	53	$6.50	$3,250	$2,291	
2030	54	$7.00	$3,500	$2,328	
2031	55	$7.00	$3,500	$2,196	
2032	56	$7.00	$7,000	$4,143	(RETIRED)
2033	57	$7.00	$7,000	$3,909	(RETIRED)
2034	58	$7.50	$7,500	$3,951	(RETIRED)
2035	59	$7.50	$7,500	$3,727	(RETIRED)
2036	60	$7.50	$7,500	$3,516	(RETIRED)
Value of Future Household Work:			$68,500	$45,293	

**POTTER V. SHRACKLE AND THE SHRACKLE CONSTRUCTION COMPANY
REBUTTAL DAMAGES MODEL OF ELIZABETH C. BUCHANAN, PhD**

**TABLE 6. FUTURE VALUE OF PERSONAL CONSUMPTION OF KATHERINE
POTTER, AGE 45 TO 60**

Date of Birth:	June 15, 1976
Date of Death:	December 4, 2021
Appraisal Period:	2023 to 2036
Projected Retirement Age:	55
Discount Rate:	6.00%
Consumption as % of Full-Time Income:	75.10%

Year	Projected Age	*Projected Value of Personal Consumption*	*Present Discounted Value of Personal Consumption*
2021	45	$63,835	
2022	46	$67,028	$67,028
2023	47	$70,381	$70,381
2024	48	$73,902	$69,719
2025	49	$77,599	$69,063
2026	50	$81,481	$68,413
2027	51	$42,778	$33,885
2028	52	$44,918	$33,566
2029	53	$47,165	$33,250
2030	54	$49,525	$32,937
2031	55	$52,002	$32,627
2032	56	(RETIRED)	(RETIRED)
2033	57	(RETIRED)	(RETIRED)
2034	58	(RETIRED)	(RETIRED)
2035	59	(RETIRED)	(RETIRED)
2036	60	(RETIRED)	(RETIRED)
Value of Future Consumption:		$606,781	$510,868

Dr. Elizabeth C. Buchanan

Business Address:
Department of Economics, DB #234
Nita State University, CB# 233
Nita City, Nita
(555) 555-4387
Fax: (555) 555-4388
Email: ebuchan@email.nsu.edu

Education:

BS University of Nita, 2007 (economics); PhD University of Nita, 2011 (economics)

Current Position:

Assistant Professor of Economics, Nita State University. Concentration in labor economics and industrial organization.

Employment History:

Assistant Professor of Economics, Nita State University since 2016. Dunhill Consultants, private economics consulting group, 2011–2016.

Principal Publications since 2011:

"The Value of Household Services," 18 *Journal of Labor Economics* 284 (2013)

"Damage Assessment for the Infringement of Intellectual Property Rights," 82 *Contemporary Economics Problems* 1204 (2017)

"Economic Loss in Copyright Cases," 4 *Journal of Law and Economics* 48 (2018)

"Can We Accurately Evaluate Lost Wages?" 7 *Journal of Law and Economics* 87 (2021)

"Intellectual Property and Modern Economic Thought," 80 *Harvard Public Policy Review* 438 (2022)

Expert Testimony:

Homer v. Underhill, Nita Superior Court, June 2016 (personal injury case, testified for the plaintiff with regard to economic loss resulting from injury)

Glandon v. Schwartz, Nita Superior Court, May 2018 (wrongful death case, testified for defendant with regard to economic loss resulting from death)

Marydale v. Farrer, Nita Superior Court, September 2021 (personal injury case, testified for the defendant with regard to economic loss resulting from injury)

MEMORANDUM

To: Robert Glenn, PhD

From: Steve Dyer, Research Assistant

Date: March 16, 2023

Re: Potter v. Shrackle

CONFIDENTIAL

Per your request, I've read through Dr. Buchanan's expert report in the Potter case. Contrasting her analysis with yours, I think the following points are important.

First, Dr. Buchanan assumes that Katherine Potter will completely stop working at age fifty-five. In his deposition, Daniel Sloan, her boss, stated that, "She told me that there was no way that she would retire before she was sixty." Dr. Buchanan doesn't address this testimony in her expert report. In fact, the deposition testimony of Jeffrey Potter indicates that, although he mentioned early retirement to her, Ms. Potter did not agree to it.

Second, Dr. Buchanan does not include the possibility that Ms. Potter might have been promoted, which would have resulted in an increase in Ms. Potter's annual salary. Mr. Sloan mentioned in his deposition that his "business is expanding" and "Ms. Potter was exactly the kind of person" the business needed because "she had all of the technical skills as well as an extraordinary ability to work with people." Mr. Sloan even goes as far as saying that he was "grooming her to become an executive vice president." This indicates that it is very likely that Ms. Potter would have been promoted before she retired and would have received a commensurate boost in her salary. Dr. Buchanan assumes that she wouldn't be promoted and her salary growth would be stagnant.

Third, Dr. Buchanan understates the value of Ms. Potter's fringe benefits as a percentage of her annual salary. She uses 17.5 percent of Ms. Potter's salary to calculate benefits. However, the actual amount of benefits, excluding the $10,000 bonus, is closer to 17.65 percent. Even though it is probably not a large difference in terms of damages, it is an inaccuracy in her report. More importantly, I believe your estimates using 20 percent for the fringe benefits package is correct. In his deposition, Daniel Sloan states, "At the time of her death, her fringe benefits package was 20 percent of her salary. This included contribution to a retirement plan, medical and dental insurance, as well as life and disability insurance." Based upon this statement, the $10,000 bonus is not included in the 20 percent which Mr. Sloan talks about. I think Dr. Buchanan was confused when she talked to Linda Graham and thought the $10,000 was included in Mr. Sloan's 20 percent figure for fringe benefits.

Fourth, Dr. Buchanan uses minimum wage as the replacement cost for the loss of Ms. Potter's household labor. Some household chores, however, should be valued at more than the minimum wage, such as cooking and gardening, as Mr. Potter really could not find somebody to do such things for minimum wage. In addition, to the extent that Ms. Potter had specialized skills (such as managing the household finances, preparing tax returns, etc.), the value of her lost work should be valued at its replacement cost, which would likely be higher than minimum wage.

On the other hand, I note in your report that you use Ms. Potter's imputed hourly wage at Techno-Soft, Inc. to value her lost household work. I think the calculation comes out to be somewhere around $41 per hour for her imputed wage. Even if Dr. Buchanan underestimates the value of Ms. Potter's lost household work using the hourly minimum wage, I think using her imputed Techno-Soft, Inc. wage may overstate the value of her lost household work insofar as it would not take someone making $41 per hour to do basic, unskilled household work.

Fifth, both you and Dr. Buchanan use the same discount rate in your calculations.

Sixth, both you and Dr. Buchanan use the same consumption rate in your calculations.

I will continue to look for more documents that can better support our arguments. In the meantime, I will come by your office later in the week so that you can approve my time sheet.

JURY INSTRUCTIONS

Preliminary Instructions

1. Introduction

You have been selected as jurors and have taken an oath to well and truly try this case. This trial will last one day.

During the progress of the trial there will be periods of time when the Court recesses. During those periods of time, you must not talk about this case among yourselves or with anyone else. Do not talk to any of the parties, their lawyers, or any of the witnesses.

You should keep an open mind. You should not form or express an opinion during the trial and should reach no conclusion in this case until you have heard all the evidence, the arguments of counsel, and the final instructions as to the law that will be given to you by the Court.

2. Conduct of the Trial

First, the attorneys will have an opportunity to make opening statements. These statements are not evidence and should be considered only as a preview of what the attorneys expect the evidence will be.

Following the opening statements, witnesses will be called to testify. They will be placed under oath and questioned by the attorneys. Documents and other tangible exhibits may also be received as evidence. If an exhibit is given to you to examine, you should examine it carefully, individually, and without any comment.

It is counsel's right and duty to object when testimony or other evidence is being offered that he or she believes is not admissible.

When the Court sustains an objection to a question, the jurors must disregard the question and the answer, if one has been given, and draw no inference from the question or answer or speculate as to what the witness would have said if permitted to answer. Jurors must also disregard evidence stricken from the record.

When the Court sustains an objection to any evidence the jurors must disregard that evidence. When the Court overrules an objection to any evidence, the jurors must not give that evidence any more weight than if the objection had not been made.

When the evidence is completed, the attorneys will make final statements. These final statements are not evidence but are given to assist you in evaluating the evidence. The attorneys are also permitted to argue in an attempt to persuade you to a particular verdict. You may accept or reject those arguments as you see fit.

Finally, just before you retire to consider your verdict, I will give you further instructions on the law that applies to this case.

FINAL INSTRUCTIONS

1. Members of the jury, the evidence and arguments in this case have been completed, and I will now instruct you as to the law.

   The laws applicable to this case are stated in these instructions and it is your duty to follow all of them. You must not single out certain instructions and disregard others.

   It is your duty to determine the facts, and to determine them only from the evidence in this case. You are to apply the law to the facts and in this way decide the case. You must not be governed or influenced by sympathy or prejudice for or against any party in this case. Your verdict must be based on evidence and not upon speculation, guess, or conjecture.

   From time to time, the court has ruled on the admissibility of evidence. You must not concern yourselves with the reasons for these rulings. You should disregard questions and exhibits that were withdrawn or to which objections were sustained.

   You should also disregard testimony and exhibits that the court has refused or stricken. The evidence that you should consider consists only of the witnesses' testimonies and the exhibits the court has received.

   Any evidence that was received for a limited purpose should not be considered by you for any other purpose.

   You should consider all the evidence in the light of your own observations and experiences in life.

   Neither by these instructions nor by any ruling or remark that I have made do I mean to indicate any opinion as to the facts or as to what your verdict should be.

2. You are the sole judges of the credibility of the witnesses and of the weight to be given to the testimony of each witness. In determining what credit is to be given any witness, you may take into account his or her ability and opportunity to observe; his or her manner and appearance while testifying; any interest, bias, or prejudice he or she may have; the reasonableness of the testimony considered in the light of all the evidence; and any other factors that bear on the believability and weight of the witness' testimony.

3. You have heard evidence in this case from witnesses who testified as experts. The law allows experts to express an opinion on subjects involving their special knowledge, training and skill, experience, or research. While their opinions are allowed to be given, it is entirely within the province of the jury to determine what weight shall be given their testimony. Jurors are not bound by the testimony of experts; their testimony is to be weighed as that of any other witness.

4. The law recognizes two kinds of evidence: direct and circumstantial. Direct evidence proves a fact directly; that is, the evidence by itself, if true, establishes the fact. Circumstantial evidence is the proof of facts or circumstances that give rise to a reasonable inference of other facts; that is, circumstantial evidence proves a fact indirectly in that it follows from other facts or circumstances according to common experience and observations in life. An eyewitness is a common example of direct evidence, while human footprints are circumstantial evidence that a person was present.

   The law makes no distinction between direct and circumstantial evidence as to the degree or amount of proof required, and each should be considered according to whatever weight or value it may have. All the evidence should be considered and evaluated by you in arriving at your verdict.

5. When I say that a party has the burden of proof on any issue, or use the expression "if you find," "if you decide," or "by a preponderance of the evidence," I mean that you must be persuaded from a consideration of all the evidence in the case that the issue in question is more probably true than not true.

   Any findings of fact you make must be based on probabilities, not possibilities. They may not be based on surmise, speculation, or conjecture.

6. One of the parties in this case is a corporation, and it is entitled to the same fair treatment as an individual would be entitled to under like circumstances, and you should decide the case with the same impartiality you would use in deciding a case between individuals.

7. The Court will now instruct you on the claims and defenses of each party and the law governing the case. You must arrive at your verdict by unanimous vote, applying the law, as you are now instructed, to the facts as you find them to be.

8. Plaintiff claims that Charles Shrackle was negligent in his operation and control of the pickup truck and that his negligence caused Katherine Potter's injuries and death. Plaintiff seeks damages for defendants' negligence both on behalf of himself individually and as the administrator of Katherine Potter's estate. Thus, plaintiff has brought this lawsuit and is claiming damages in two separate capacities: (1) as an individual for the injury and loss suffered by him as Katherine Potter's husband, and (2) as the administrator of Katherine Potter's estate for the pain, suffering, and expenses incurred by her prior to her death.

   Defendants deny that Charles Shrackle was negligent or that his negligence caused Katherine Potter's injuries and death. Defendants claim that Katherine Potter was negligent, and that it was her own negligence that caused her injuries and death.

9. In this case, the plaintiff, Jeffrey Potter, has the burden of proving:

   (1)   That Charles Shrackle was negligent, and;

   (2)   That the negligence of Charles Shrackle proximately caused Katherine Potter's death.

   The defendants have the burden of proving:

   (1)   That the deceased, Katherine Potter, was negligent, and;

   (2)   That the negligence of Katherine Potter was a proximate cause of her death.

   Thus, each of the parties to this case has a burden of proof to maintain, and you are to determine whether they have met their burdens. Your task is to determine whether Charles Shrackle or Katherine Potter, or both, were negligent, and the extent to which their negligence caused Katherine Potter's injuries and death.

10. The terms "negligent" or "negligence" as used in these instructions mean the failure to use that degree of care that an ordinarily careful and prudent person would use under the same or similar circumstances.

11. The terms "contributorily negligent" or "contributory negligence" mean negligence on the part of the deceased Katherine Potter.

12. It is the duty of every person using a public street or highway, whether a pedestrian or a driver of a vehicle, to exercise ordinary care to avoid placing himself, herself, or others in danger and to exercise ordinary care to avoid a collision.

13. The violation of a statute, if you find any, is negligence as a matter of law. Such negligence has the same effect as any other act or acts of negligence.

    A statute in the state of Nita provides:

    (1) That the driver of a motor vehicle shall yield the right of way, by slowing down or stopping if necessary, to a pedestrian crossing the roadway within a crosswalk when the pedestrian is upon that half of the roadway in which the vehicle is traveling, or when either the vehicle or the pedestrian is approaching that half of the roadway so closely that the pedestrian is in danger.

    (2) That a pedestrian crossing a roadway at any point other than within a marked crosswalk shall yield the right of way to all vehicles upon the roadway.

    (3) This right of way, however, is not absolute but rather creates a duty to exercise ordinary care to avoid collisions upon the party having the right of way.

14. Proximate cause is that cause which, in a natural and continuous sequence, produces the injury, and without which the injury would not have occurred.

    To be a proximate cause of Katherine Potter's injuries and death, negligent conduct by either Charles Shrackle or Katherine Potter need not be the only cause, nor the last or nearest cause. It is sufficient if the negligent conduct acting concurrently with another cause produced the injury.

    Thus, there need not be only one proximate cause of Katherine Potter's injuries and death, and you may find that the negligence of both Charles Shrackle and Katherine Potter was the proximate cause of her death. On the other hand, you may find that the negligence of either of them was the sole proximate cause of her death.

15. You are to determine the negligence, if any, of both Charles Shrackle and Katherine Potter, and then to apportion the responsibility of each.

    Please state your findings of negligence in the following form:

    We find the conduct of the defendant, Charles Shrackle, was_____% negligent.

    We find that the conduct of the deceased, Katherine Potter, was _____% negligent.

16. In this case you must also decide the issue of damages. You must determine the amount which will reasonably and fairly compensate Jeffrey Potter for the losses resulting from the death of his wife, Katherine Potter.

    In determining the loss to the plaintiff, Jeffrey Potter, you should consider the following factors:

    (1) Expenses for care, treatment, and hospitalization incident to the injury to Katherine Potter resulting in her death;

    (2) Compensation for the pain and suffering of the decedent;

    (3) The reasonable funeral expenses of the decedent;

    (4) The present monetary value of the decedent to the persons entitled to receive the damages recovered, including but not limited to compensation for the loss of the reasonably expected:

        (a) net income of the decedent;

    (b)   services, protection, care, and assistance of the decedent, whether voluntary or obligatory, to the persons entitled to the damages recovered;

    (c)   society, companionship, comfort, guidance, kindly offices, and advice of the decedent to the persons entitled to the damages recovered; and

(5)   Nominal damages when the jury so finds.

17. In determining the amount of damages to the plaintiff, you may consider how long the plaintiff is likely to live, how long the decedent was likely to have lived, that some persons work all their lives and others do not, that a person's earnings may remain the same or may increase or decrease in the future.

In calculating the amount of damages, you must not simply multiply the life expectancies by the annual damages. Instead, you must determine the present cash value for any award of damages. "Present cash value" means the sum of money needed now, which together with what that sum will earn in the future, will equal the amount of the benefits at the times in the future when they would have been received.

18. The Court did not in any way, and does not by these instructions, give or intimate any opinions as to what has or has not been proven in the case, or as to what are or are not the facts of the case.

No one of these instructions states all the law applicable, but all of them must be taken, read, and considered together as they are connected with and related to each other as a whole.

You must not be concerned with the wisdom of any rule of law. Regardless of any opinions you may have as to what the law ought to be, it would be a violation of your sworn duty to base a verdict upon any other view of the law than that given in the instructions of the court.

IN THE CIRCUIT COURT OF
DARROW COUNTY, NITA
CIVIL DIVISION

Jeffrey T. Potter, the Administrator of the Estate, and of Katherine Potter, Jeffrey T. Potter, individually,	)))))	
Plaintiffs,	))	Jury Verdict (Interrogatories)
v.	)))	
Charles T. Shrackle and The Shrackle Construction Company,	)))	
Defendants.	))	

The jury is to answer the following interrogatories. The foreperson is to answer the interrogatories for the jury and sign the verdict.

Interrogatory No. 1:

Please state your findings of negligence in the following form:

We find that the conduct of the defendant, Charles T. Shrackle, was _____% negligent.

We find that the conduct of the deceased, Katherine Potter, was _____% negligent.

Interrogatory No. 2:

Please determine the amount of damages to the plaintiff, Jeffrey T. Potter, both individually and as administrator of Katherine Potter's estate:

Amount $_____

The percentage of negligence that you find to be apportioned to the defendant, Charles T. Shrackle (Interrogatory No. 1) is multiplied by the amount of damages you determine (Interrogatory No. 2), and that amount will be the verdict for the plaintiff, Jeffrey T. Potter.

The members of the jury have unanimously answered the interrogatories in the manner that I have indicated.

_____

Foreperson

EXHIBITS

| Department of Transportation Bureau of Safety Programing and Analysis T&S Building, Nita City, Nita | **NITA POLICE DEPARTMENT TRAFFIC ACCIDENT REPORT** | Page 1 of 2 |

Investigating Officer/ Badge No.	Michael Young / #7319	Date of Report	12/4/21	Approved By/ Date	
Date	11/30/21	Time	3:28	County	Darrow	City	Nita City
No. Vehicles	1	No. Killed	1	No. Injuried		Municipality	

Principal Road

Street Name: Mattis   Speed Limit:

Nearest Cross Street: Kirby

Intersecting Road

Street Name: Speed Limit:

Check if One Way: ☐ N ☐ S ☐ E ☐ W

Direction From Accident Site: ☐ N ☐ S ☐ E ☐ W

Illumination	Weather	Road Surface	Traffic Control Device Type
☐ Dawn or Dusk	☒ No Adverse Conditions	☒ Dry	☐ No Controls ☐ RR Crossing Controls
☒ Daylight	☐ Raining	☐ Wet	☐ Flashing Traffic Signal ☐ Police Officer/Flagman
☐ Dark (with street lights)	☐ Sleet/Hail	☐ Muddy	☒ Traffic Signal ☐ Flashing School Zone Sign
☐ Dark (with no street lights)	☐ Snowing	☐ Snow/Ice	☐ Stop Sign ☐ Other
	☐ Fog/Smoke		☐ Yield Sign

Vehicle Driver No. 1

☒ Moving ☐ Stopped in Traffic ☐ Parked ☐ Pedestrian ☐ Bicyclist ☐ Other

Drivers Name: Charles T. Shrackle   Divers License Number: State:

Street Address: 1701 W Johnston   Date of Birth: 5/13/73

City: Nita City State: Nita Zip Code: Telephone Numbers:

Vehicle (Year/Make): 2001 Toyota pickup License Plate or ID Number: State: Nita

Vehicle Owner: Charles T. Shrackle   Date of Birth:

Address: City: State: Zip Code:

Vehicle Driver No. 2

☐ Moving ☐ Stopped in Traffic ☐ Parked ☒ Pedestrian ☐ Bicyclist ☐ Other

Drivers Name: Katherine Potter   Divers License Number: State:

Street Address: 4920 Thorndale Avenue   Date of Birth:

City: Nita City State: Nita Zip Code: Telephone Numbers:

Vehicle (Year/Make): License Plate or ID Number: State:

Vehicle Owner: Date of Birth:

Address: City: State: Zip Code:

Department of Transportation
Bureau of Safety
Programing and Analysis
T&S Building, Nita City, Nita

NITA POLICE DEPARTMENT TRAFFIC ACCIDENT REPORT

Page 2 of 2

Witnesses

(A) Juanita and Vicky Williams
    1010 W Kirby #15
    Nita

(B) Marilyn Kelly
    1910 Elden Lane
    Nita

Narrative

#1 was southbound on Mattis after turning left from Kirby. He then struck #2 (pedestrian) approx 30 feet S of pedestrian crosswalk. #1 said he didn't see pedestrian until after he struck her. Witnesses A (mother & daughter) had been in car driving east on Kirby and saw pedestrian running across street westbound. Neither saw actual contact.

On 12/1/21 witness B called station and said pedestrian was in crosswalk.

On 12/4/21 I was informed that pedestrian had died.

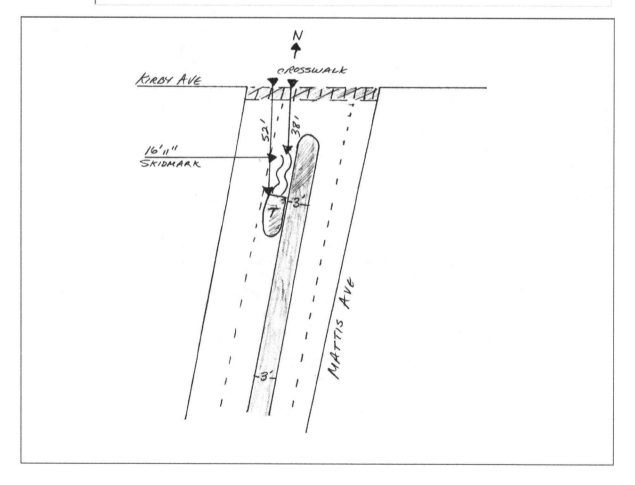

Exhibit 2

MAPS OF MATTIS AND KIRBY AVENUE AREA

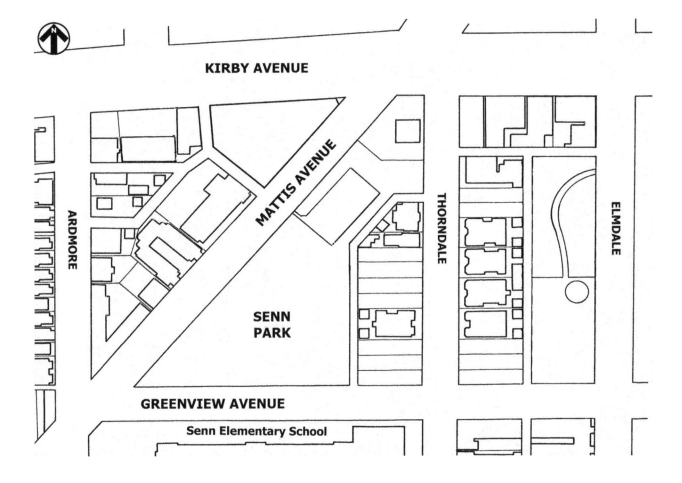

KIRBY AVENUE

MATTIS AVENUE

ARDMORE

THORNDALE

ELMDALE

SENN
PARK

GREENVIEW AVENUE

Senn Elementary School

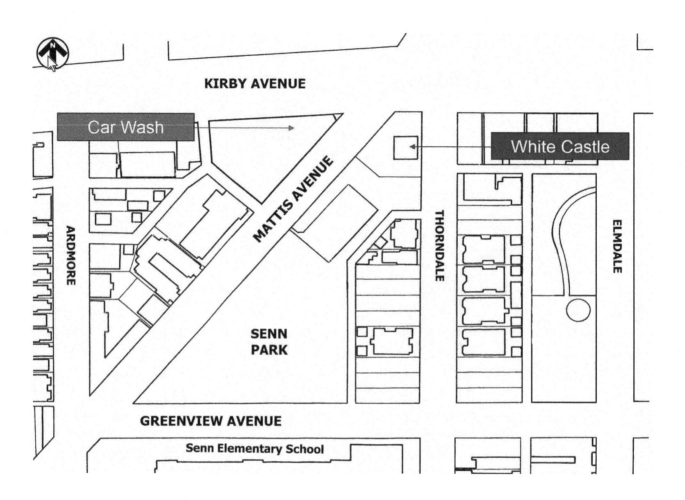

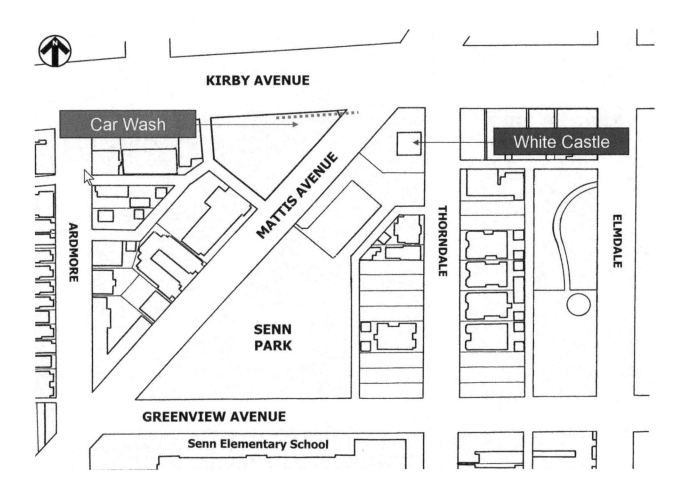

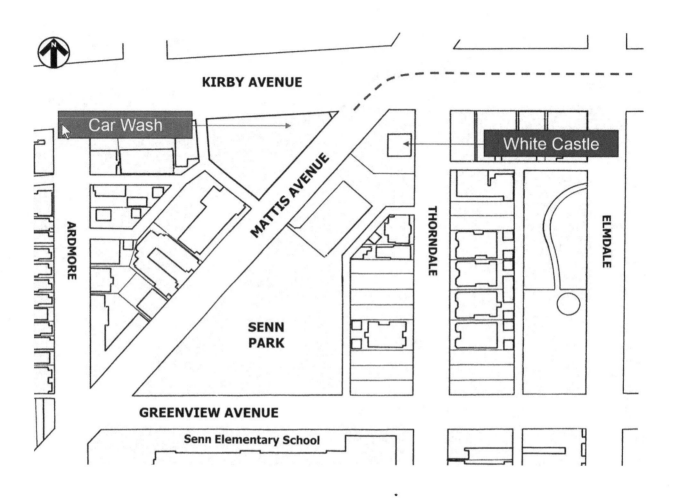

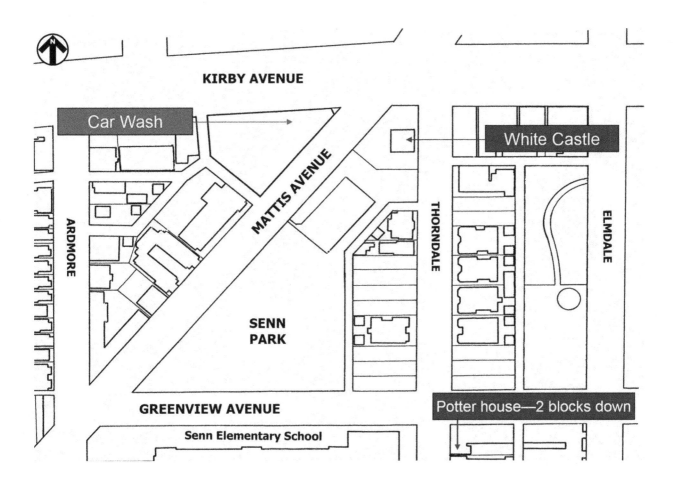

Exhibit 3

CLOSE-UP STREET DIAGRAMS OF MATTIS AND KIRBY AVENUE AREA

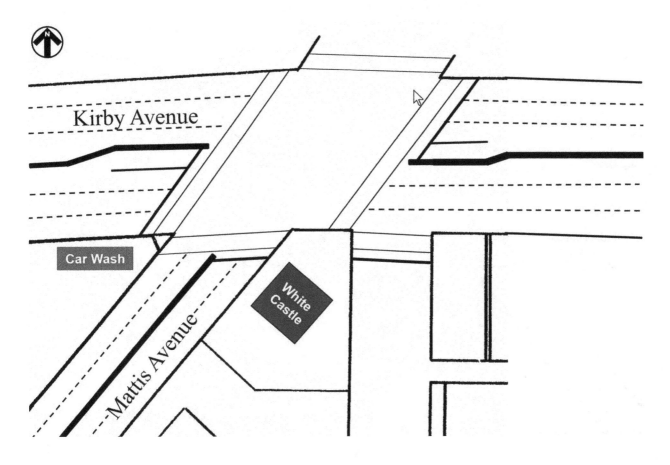

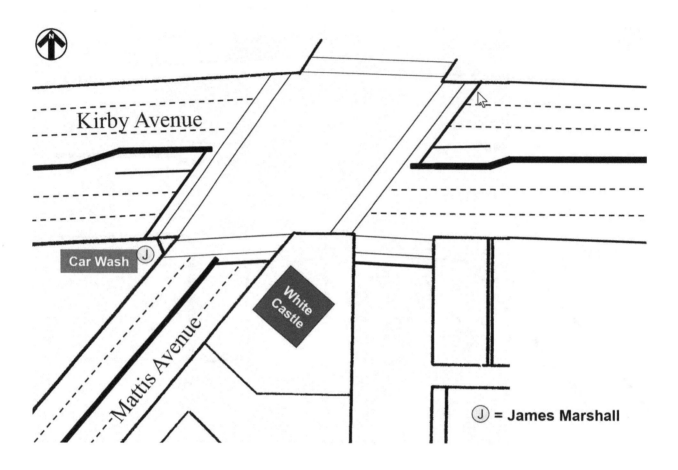

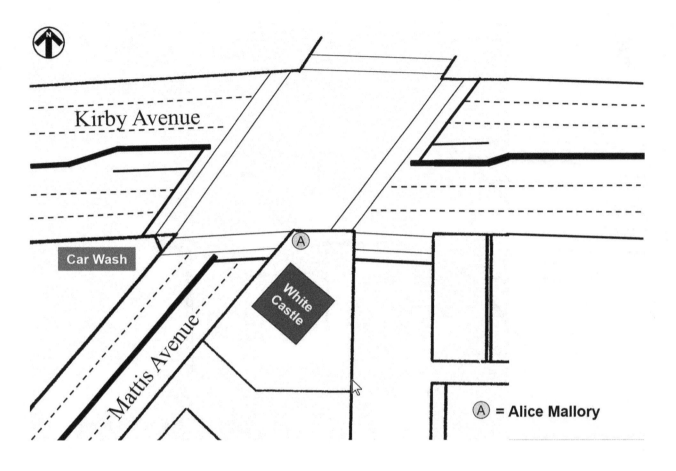

Exhibit 3c

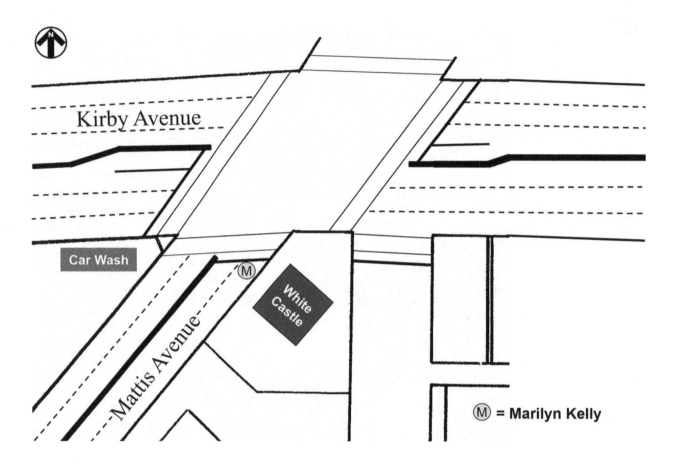

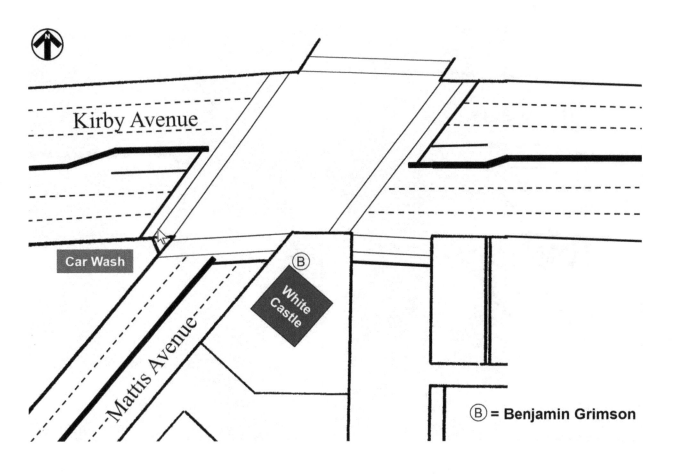

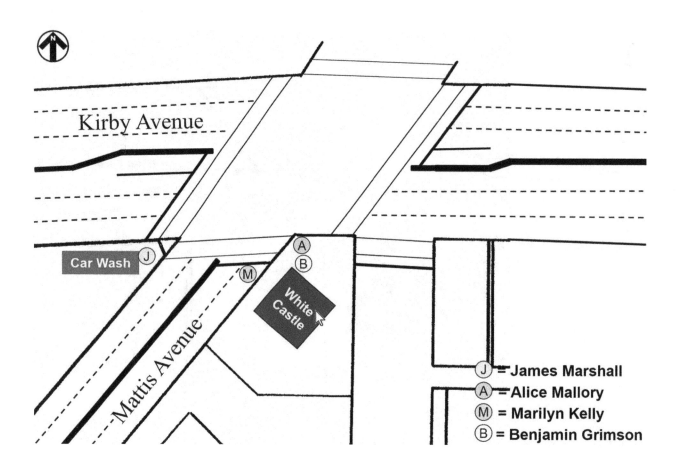

Exhibit 4

PHOTO OF KATHRINE POTTER AFTER BEING STUCK BY CHARLES POTTER'S CAR

Exhibit 5

PHOTO OF KATHRINE POTTER WHEN SHE WAS ALIVE

Exhibit 6

PHOTO OF CHARLES SHRACKLE BY HIS TRUCK

Exhibit 7

PHOTO OF SHRACKLE CONSTRUCTION TRUCK

Exhibit 8

CLOSE-UP PHOTO OF SHRACKLE CONSTRUCTION LOGO ON TRUCK

Exhibit 9

VIEW FROM CAR WASH EAST TOWARD WHITE CASTLE—DIAGRAMS AND PHOTOS

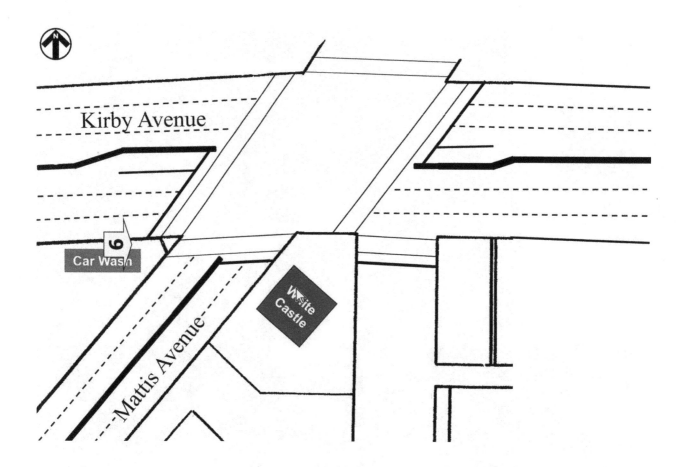

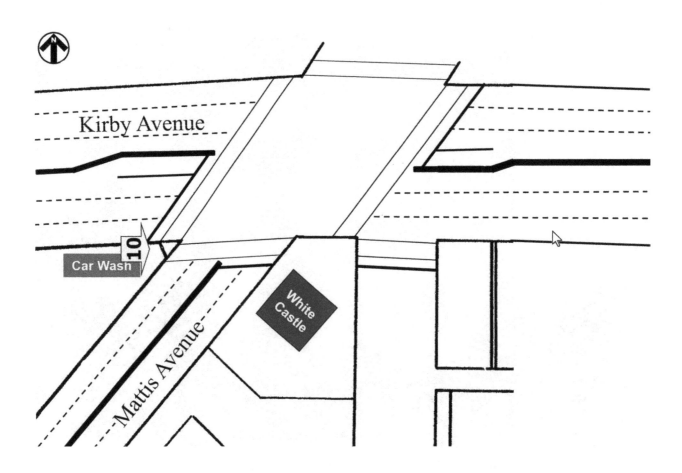

Exhibit 11

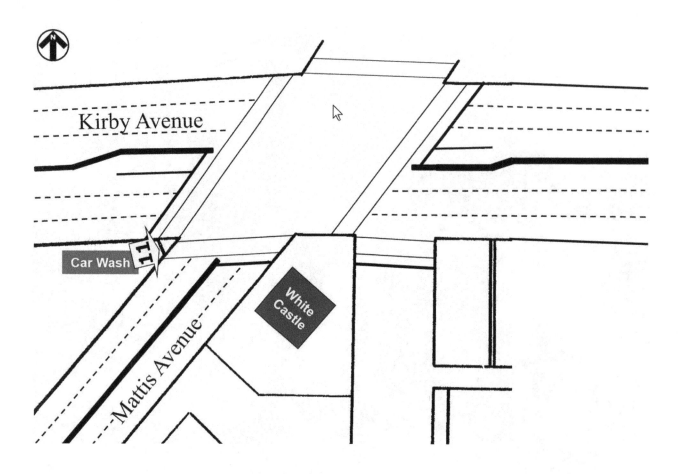

Exhibit 12

VIEW FROM WHITE CASTLE WEST TOWARD CAR WASH—DIAGRAMS AND PHOTOS

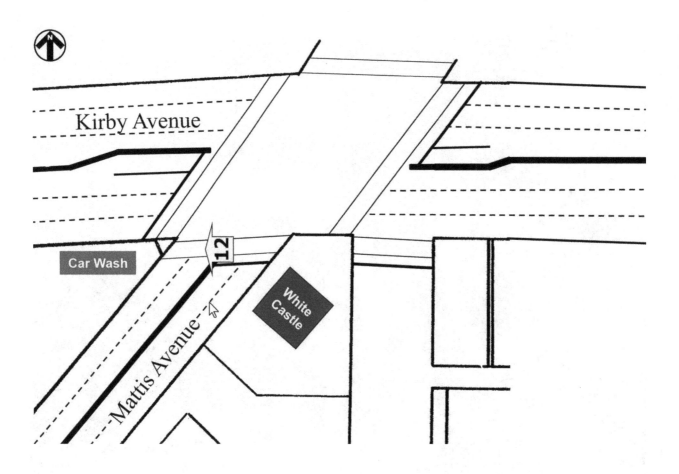

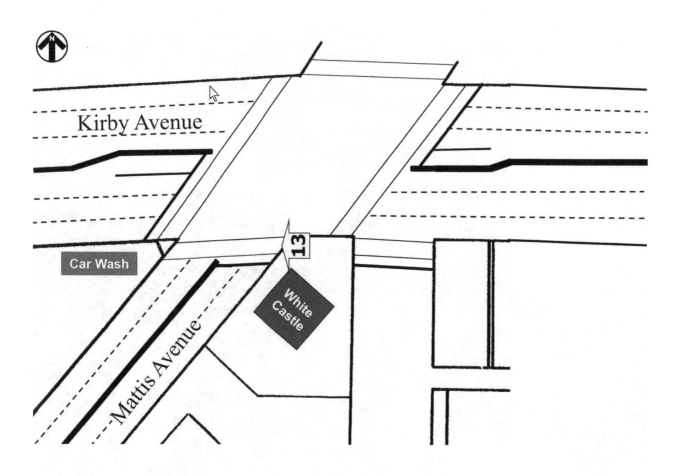

View of Mattis Avenue Median Looking Southwest—Diagram and Photo

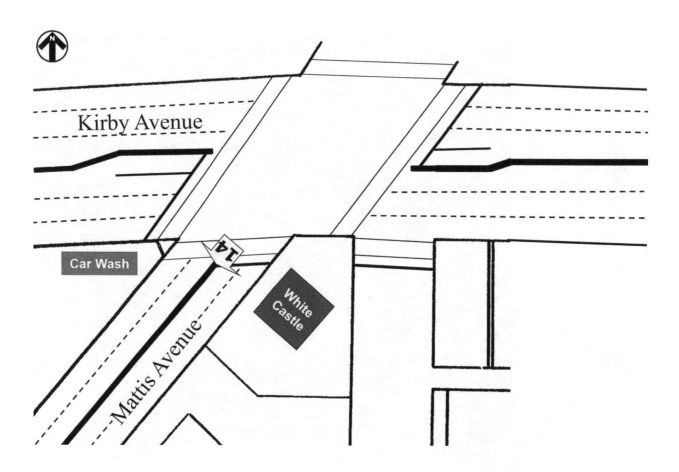

Exhibit 15

VIEW OF MATTIS AVENUE MEDIAN LOOKING NORTHEAST—DIAGRAM AND PHOTO

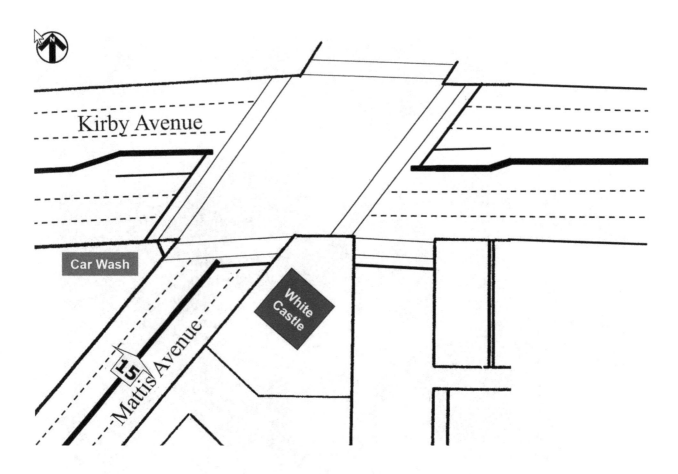

Exhibit 16

VIEWS FROM KIRBY AVENUE MEDIAN LOOKING WEST AND SOUTHWEST—DIAGRAMS AND PHOTOS

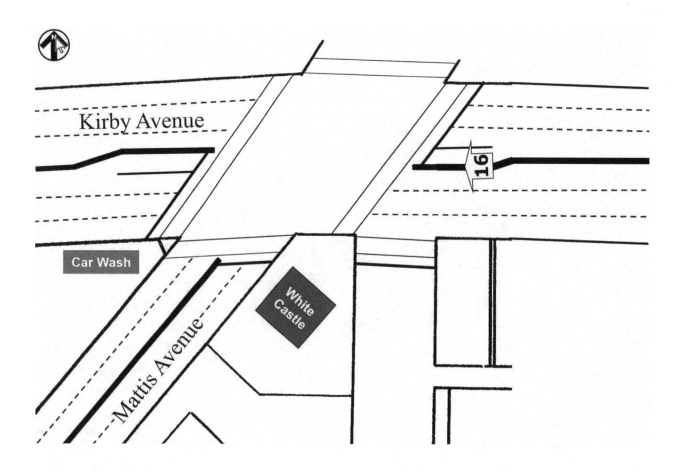

Exhibit 17 (cont'd)

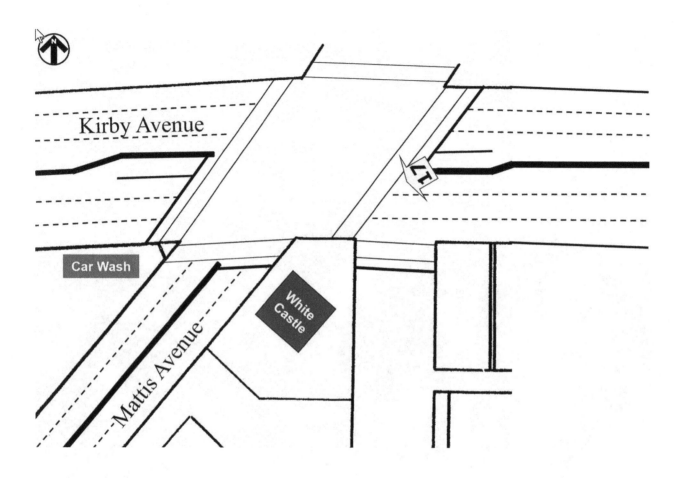

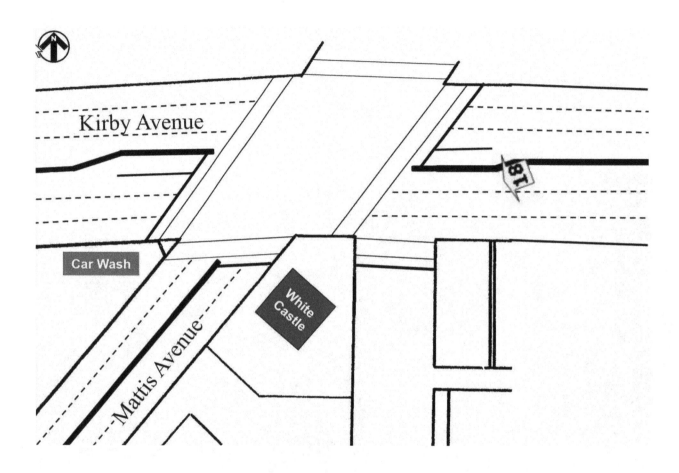

Exhibit 19

VIEWS FROM WHITE CASTLE DRIVE-THRU KIRBY AVENUE AND MATTIS AVENUE INTERSECTION— DIAGRAMS AND PHOTOS

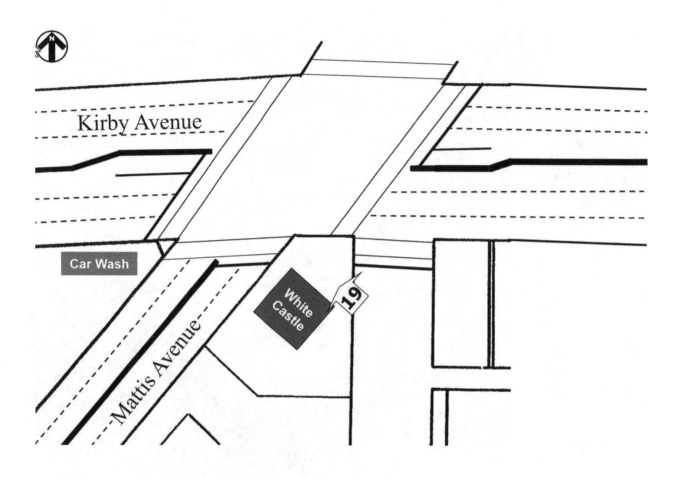

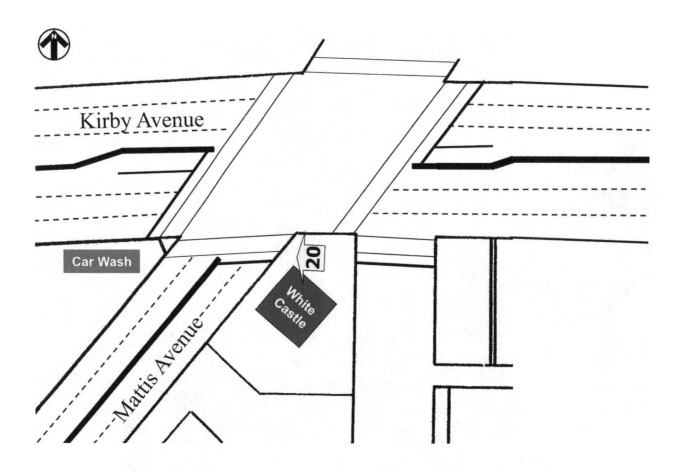

Exhibit 21

VIEW FROM WHITE CASTLE DRIVE-THRU ACROSS MATTIS AVENUE TOWARD CAR WASH–DIAGRAM AND PHOTO

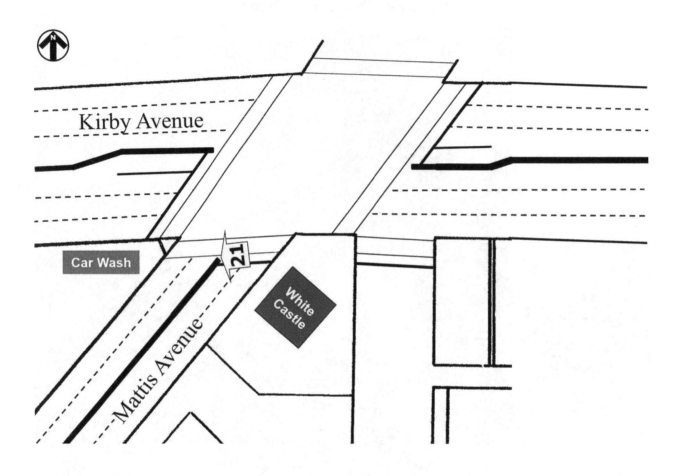

Exhibit 22[1]

STATEMENT OF JAMES MARSHALL

Statement of James Marshall

I am the owner-operator of Jim Marshall's tires, 1601 ~~1610~~ Kirby, Nita City, Nita. I was working in the car wash portion of my business on Nov. 30, 2021

At approximately 3:30 on Nov. 30, 2021, I was doing some maintenance work on one of the vacuum units for the car wash. It was the ~~first~~ second from the corner. I saw a dark-haired woman walking east on the south sidewalk of KIRBY. When I saw her, she was 15 or 20 feet from the intersection. I looked over at my employee, Ed Putnam, to ask him something about the job we were doing. About a minute or minute and a half later I heard a thump. I looked out and saw a pickup truck carrying a body on the front of it. I sent Putnam out to see if he could be of help while I called the police. I went out to see if I could be of help and saw the same woman that I'd seen earlier walking east on KIRBY lying on the pavement.

Signed: James Marshall
Witness: Joseph Lucey
Dec. 12, 2021

---

1. Marshall's business is located on the southwest corner of Kirby and Mattis. This statement was taken by Joseph Lucey, an adjuster for the defendant's insurance carrier, on December 8, 2021, at about 11 a.m. The statement was written by Mr. Lucey. The signature and the correction are in Marshall's handwriting.

Exhibit 23

EMAIL FROM CLARK POE TO CHARLES SHRACKLE NOVEMBER 29, 2021

Charles Shrackle

From:	Clark Poe <cpoe@poecon.nita>
Sent:	Monday, November 29, 2021 9:34 AM
To:	Charles Shrackle
Subject:	Greenbriar

Charlie: The delays on the Greenbriar project are unacceptable. We are so far behind that the developer, Mr. Green, is about ready to cancel the job and get a new contractor. Legally, he can probably do it.

I know that you've had some trouble with rock, but there is always trouble with rock in this area. We need to finish this job immediately!

Come to the job site at 3:30 p.m. tomorrow and be ready to give me a detailed description of your problems and a firm commitment on a conclusion date. This has become a real problem, Charlie, so be there and be on time.

Clark

Clark Poe Construction Company
414 Whitebread Road
Nita City, Nita 99992
(555) 828-1891
cpoe@poecon.nita

Exhibit 24

EMAIL FROM CHARLES SHRACKLE TO CLARK POE NOVEMBER 29, 2021

Charles T. Shrackle

From:	Charles T. Shrackle <cts@shrackleconstruction.nita>
Sent:	Monday, November 29, 2021 10:23 AM
To:	Clark Poe (cpoe@poecon.nita)
Subject:	Greenbriar

Clark: I hear you loud and clear. I'll be there at 3:30 tomorrow. Unlike sometimes in the past, I assure you I won't be late.

Charlie

Charles T. Shrackle
Shrackle Construction Company
Route 45
Sommers Township
Nita City, Nita 99994
(555) 826-9406

Exhibit 25

WEATHER REPORT FOR NITA CITY, NOVEMBER 30, 2021

Nita City Weather Channel
www.ncweather.nita

Weather report for Nita City, Nita on November 30, 2021

Sunny
56°
Chance of Rain: 0%
Wind: W at 11 mph
Sunny skies. High 56F. Winds W at 10 to 15 mph.

Sunrise: 6:55 am	**Sunset:** 4:21 pm

Exhibit 26

NITA MEMORIAL HOSPITAL STATEMENT FOR KATHERINE POTTER, DATED DECEMBER 7, 2021

NMH Nita Memorial Hospital

444 Medway Park Circle Nita City, Nita 57818

(819)555-0101   www.nmh.nita

SF-1 Statement

Please note: This is a short form statement listing general chares. Itemization statements are available upon request for all services and goods provided.

Statement date:	**12/7/2021**
Patient:	**Katherine Potter (deceased)**
Patient ID:	**4478-622-00**
Admitted:	**Yes**
Time/date of initial treatment	**4:18 p.m. 11/30/2021**
ER attending physician	**Ashley P. Smith, MD, #609**
Other physician(s):	**Kevin M. Patterson, MD, #711**
Brief Description:	**Severe head trauma, brain injury, and fractured skill; result of being struck by moving vehicle. Intermittent consciousness; surgery to relieve pressure on brain**
Release date:	**T O D 12/4/2021 4:00 p.m.**

Date	Description	Amount
11/30/2021	**NMH Ambulance Service**	$840
11/30/2021	**Emergency Room**	$4,500
	ER physician (Ref: Ashley P. Smith, MD, #609)	$5,080
	Medications administered	$1,660
12/01/2021	**Physician, surgery, medications; tests; blood, IV**	$11,720
12/04/2021	**Intensive care private room and attendant care**	$84,200
	5 days @$17,000	
12/4/2021	**NMH morgue service**	$800
	Total	$107,800

Exhibit 27

ODELL FUNERAL HOME STATEMENT, DATED JANUARY 12, 2022

Odell Funeral Home

2002 Eternity Way, Nita City, Nita 57823

(819) 555-2789

Confidential Invoice

INVOICE DATE   January 12, 2022
SERVICES FOR: Katherine Potter, December 11, 2021

20-gauge reinforced "Norabella" casket, sealed	$8000
Heavy duty gasket, screw lock, seal kit	229
Delivery included	
General prep services	600
Additional prep	200
Silk flower casket spray (blue, white, gold)	200
Memorial stone	2,300
Photo etched	375
"Restful Garden" Mausoleum, unit 40	3,000
Peace Garden Cemetery, Nita City,	980
service fee	
Limousine 2 hours @ $270.50/hour	541
10-inch obituary in Nita Journal-Gazette with photo	75
TOTAL DUE, NET 30:	**$16,500**

Exhibit 28

Jeffrey Potter Letter to Dr. Andrew Stevens, dated September 2, 2021

4920 Thorndale Avenue
Nita City, Nita 99993
September 2, 2021

Dr. Andrew Stevens
Stevens Counseling
1225 North Street
Lisle, Nita 99980

Dear Dr. Stevens:

I am sorry that payment for our last three sessions is late. I guess it goes without saying that Katherine and I don't see eye to eye on the need for this counseling, and it is very difficult for me to get her to even speak calmly about it, much less agree for us to pay for it. Nonetheless, I am enclosing our check in the amount of $300.

I am sorry that we can't continue with you. I thought your advice was very helpful and I appreciated the opportunity to talk with you about the problems that we have been having. I especially want to thank you for your concern about the early retirement issue. Even though Katherine loves her career, I am confident she would like the leisurely life of a college professor's wife even more. When we first got married, I was unable to talk her into having children. She was too career-driven. I hope that I can make more headway on the retirement issue.

Your comments at the last session that it was obvious to you that Katherine and I loved each other very much, and would come out of this stronger than ever, make me smile and look forward to the future. I am sure that you are right. Perhaps when we have more time and her career isn't so hectic, I'll be able to persuade Katherine to come back with me to talk to you about the rest of our problems, which don't seem quite so important now. Despite all the difficulties, I believe that our marriage will work. If it doesn't, so be it. If we can't resolve things, I can leave the marriage and seek a relationship that fulfills my needs.

In any event, keep your fingers crossed for us, please.

Sincerely yours,
Jeffrey T. Potter

Exhibit 29

WILLIAM JAMES LETTER TO JAMES BARBER REGARDING JEFFREY POTTER'S RELATIONSHIP WITH
CHERYL TOBIAS, DATED SEPTEMBER 18, 2023

Madden & James

Suite 720 Nita Bank Building, Nita City, Nita 99994 (555) 555-0003

James Barber
Pierce, Johnson & Clark
Nita National Bank Plaza
Nita City, Nita 99994

September 18, 2023
Re: Potter v. Shrackle and Shrackle Construction Co.
Jim:

Although I think there is no obligation to do this under the Rules, I thought I would update Jeffrey Potter's answers at his deposition with regard to his relationship with Cheryl Tobias. If asked about that relationship at this point, Mr. Potter would state:

I began a relationship with Cheryl Tobias in the late spring of 2022. That relationship ended in December 2022. The basis for ending the relationship was that I was unable to move on to another long-term relationship after the death of my wife. Cheryl and I agreed it would be better to break off the relationship at that point.

I would be happy to sign a request to admit to this effect.

Sincerely,

William James

William James

LEARNED TREATISE: *PRIMARY OPEN-ANGLE GLAUCOMA*

PRIMARY OPEN-ANGLE GLAUCOMA

Open-angle glaucoma is the most common form of glaucoma. It is also known as "primary" or "chronic" glaucoma and accounts for at least ninety percent of all glaucoma cases. "Open-angle" is used to denote that the angle where the iris meets the cornea is as open and wide as it should be. This condition affects about three million Americans and occurs mainly in people over fifty.

There are no noticeable symptoms with primary open-angle glaucoma. The eye's intraocular pressure (IOP) slowly increases and the cornea adapts without swelling. The IOP increases either when too much aqueous humor fluid (transparent, watery fluid containing low protein concentrations) is produced or by a decrease in aqueous humor outflow. The trabecular meshwork (tissue located around the base of the cornea) is responsible for most of the outflow of aqueous humor. Swelling is an indicator that something is wrong; without it, the disease often goes undetected. Patients do not feel pain and often do not realize there is an issue until the later stages of the disease and a loss of vision.

The increased pressure in the eye ultimately destroys optic nerve cells. Once enough of the nerve cells are destroyed, blind spots begin to form in the patient's field of vision. The blind spots usually start in the peripheral (outer areas) field of vision. As the disease progresses, the central vision also becomes affected. Once the vision is impaired, the damage is irreversible. There is currently no treatment to restore the dead nerve cells.

Primary open-angle glaucoma is a chronic disease. There is currently no cure for it, but the disease can be slowed through treatment. There are medications, when taken regularly that can be crucial to preventing further damage to a patient's vision. Eye drops generally are the initial treatment as they can reduce IOP by decreasing aqueous production or increasing aqueous outflow. If the patient does not respond to medication, then surgery will be indicated.

There is no visible abnormality of the trabecular meshwork. It is believed that the ability of the cells in the trabecular meshwork to carry out their normal function is compromised. It is also possible that there may be fewer cells in the meshwork as a natural result of getting older. Others believe it is because of a structural defect in the eye's drainage system or that the condition is caused by an enzymatic problem. All of these theories are currently being studied at various research centers.

 **NMJ** NITA Medical Journal   May 2017

JAMES MARSHALL TEXT, NOVEMBER 30, 2021

CHARLES SHRACKLE TEXT TO CLARK POE, NOVEMBER 30, 2021

Exhibit 33

PORTION OF CHARLES SHRACKLE PHONE BILL, NOVEMBER 21, 2021 TO DECEMBER 11, 2021

Billing period Nov 12, 2021 to Dec 11, 2021| Account # 1111101-00001 | Invoice # 123456789

Charles T. Shrackle

555.123.4567 | Nita City

Talk activity—continued

Date	Time	Number	Origination	Destination	Min.	Airtime Charges
Nov 21	3:23 PM	555.749.3112	Nita City, NITA	Nita City, NITA	1	--
Nov 22	3:31 PM	555.749.3112	Nita City, NITA	Nita City, NITA	31	--
Nov 23	12:26 PM	800.234.7350	Nita City, NITA	Nita City, NITA	7	--
Nov 24	1:31 PM	555.537.3232	Nita City, NITA	Incoming, NITA	22	--
Nov 24	10:29 AM	800.546.7800	Nita City, NITA	Toll-Free, NITA	22	--
Nov 24	10:50 AM	800.546.7800	Nita City, NITA	Toll-Free, NITA	1	--
Nov 24	10:51 AM	800.546.7800	Nita City, NITA	Toll-Free, NITA	13	--
Nov 24	12:25 PM	800.546.7800	Nita City, NITA	Toll-Free, NITA	49	--
Nov 25	2:58 PM	555.474.5612	Nita City, NITA	Nita City, NITA	1	--
Nov 25	3:24 PM	555.353.6600	Nita City, NITA	Nita City, NITA	2	--
Nov 26	11:40 AM	555.906.9330	Nita City, NITA	Nita City, NITA	12	--
Nov 26	2:26 PM	555.400.4453	Nita City, NITA	Nita City, NITA	2	--
Nov 27	4:30 PM	800.234.7350	Nita City, NITA	Toll-Free, NITA	11	--
Nov 28	4:48 PM	555.400.4453	Nita City, NITA	Incoming, NITA	31	--
Nov 29	7:22 AM	800.424.2449	Nita City, NITA	Toll-Free, NITA	11	--
Nov 30	3:28 PM	555.227.4786	Nita City, NITA	Nita City, NITA	2	--
Dec 1	11:40 AM	555.474.5612	Nita City, NITA	Nita City, NITA	14	--
Dec 2	10:28 AM	555.474.5612	Nita City, NITA	Incoming, NITA	9	--
Dec 2	5:31 PM	555.493.0494	Nita City, NITA	Nita City, NITA	1	--

Exhibit 34

DUDLEY INVESTIGATIONS MEMO TO JAMES BARBER REGARDING JUANITA WILLIAMS'S VEHICLE

DUDLEY INVESTIGATIONS

765 NITA AVENUE

NITA CITY, NITA **99994**

Memo to File: Potter v. Shrackle

Dated: December 20, 2022

Re: Vehicle driven by witness Juanita Williams
             and Shrackle Phone Record

cc: James Barber
             Pierce, Johnson & Clark
             Nita National Bank Plaza
             Nita City, Nita 99994

The three attached photos are of the front end, back end, and view out the back from the back seat of a 2019 Toyota Highlander, which is the same make, model, and year as the vehicle driven by witness Juanita Williams on November 30, 2021.

I also contacted the client and asked for his cell phone record for November 2021, which he provided and is attached.

S. Dudley, Investigator

Exhibit 34a

PHOTOS OF JUANITA WILLIAMS'S VEHICLE

Exhibit 35

DUDLEY INVESTIGATIONS MEMO TO JAMES BARBER REGARDING JEFFREY POTTER'S RELATIONSHIP WITH CHERYL TOBIAS

DUDLEY INVESTIGATIONS

765 NITA AVENUE

NITA CITY, NITA 99994

Memo to File: Potter v. Shrackle

Dated: January 15, 2023

Re: Mr. Potter's relationship with Cheryl Tobias

cc: James Barber
              Pierce, Johnson & Clark
              Nita National Bank Plaza
              Nita City, Nita 99994

As part of my investigation, I went to the campus of the University of Nita to see what I might find out about plaintiff, Professor Jeffrey Potter. In talking to people around the Physics Department, I discovered there might be more to the relationship between Professor Potter and Graduate Student Cheryl Tobias than meets the eye. A close friend of Ms. Tobias, who asked to remain anonymous, told me she was upset with how this professor used his superior position at the University to engage in an improper sexual relationship with a female underling. She said she had counselled Ms. Tobias against entering into this relationship to no avail. When I asked her if she had proof of this relationship, she took out her smartphone and showed me several ImageGram postings she had received from her friend after a trip she took with Professor Potter to Martinique earlier this year. I explained who I was and what my role was in this litigation and asked if she would be willing to do a screen grab of these various postings and email them to me. She enthusiastically replied yes and sent me five ImageGram postings, which I have printed out and attached. I told her I would do everything I could to keep her and her identity out of this lawsuit.

SCREEN CAPTURES OF CHERYL TOBIAS'S IMAGEGRAM ACCOUNT, JUNE 2022

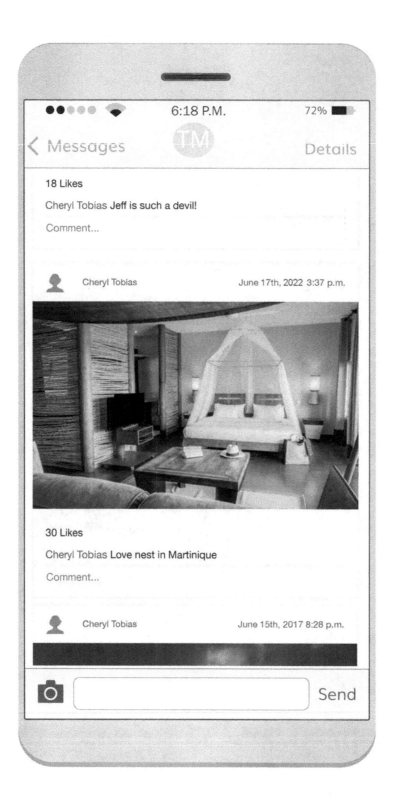

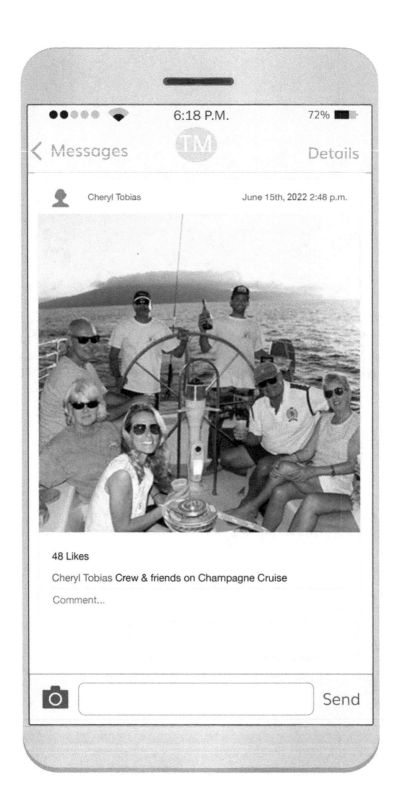

Exhibit 36

NITA TRAVEL COMPANY eTICKET RECEIPT FOR PASSENGER JEFFREY POTTER, JUNE 14, 2022

NITA TRAVEL COMPANY eTICKET RECEIPT

Reservation Code:	WQMFKA	Issuing Agent:	Nita City, Nita
Ticket Number:	8675309502425	Issuing Agent:	3BA78/4076
Issuing Airline:	CARIBBEAN AIRLINES	IATA number:	66397478
Date Issued:	30May22	Invoice number:	483228
Customer Number:	8972509574		
Passenger:	Jeffrey Potter		

14JUN22   Caribbean Air CA 1066   Seat 15B
From: Nita City, Nita (Nita City Intern'l)   Departs: 730A   Business Confirmed
To: Fort de France, Martinique (FDF)   Arrives: 355P   Fare Basis: TC8BX
                                                                                    Not Valid Before: 14JUN
                                                                                    Not Valid After: 14JUN

19JUN22   Caribbean Air CA 3631
From: Fort de France, Martinique (FDF)   Departs: 1150A   Business Confirmed
To: Nita City, Nita (Nita City Intern'l)   Arrives: 820P   Fare Basis: TC8BX
                                                                                    Not Valid Before: 19JUN
                                                                                    Not Valid After: 19JUN

Form of Payment: Credit Card - Visa - Charged to Jeffrey Potter

Endorsement/Restrictions: Nonref/Change Fee Plus Fare Diff Applies/Valid US Only

Positive Identification Required for Airport Check-In

Carriage and other service provided by the carrier are subject to conditions of carriage, which are hereby incorporated by reference. These conditions may be obtained from the issuing carrier.

Nita Travel Company . . . Your Gateway to Fun in the Sun!

Exhibit 37

NITA TRAVEL COMPANY eTICKET RECEIPT FOR PASSENGER CHERYL TOBIAS, JUNE 14, 2022

NITA TRAVEL COMPANY eTICKET RECEIPT

Reservation Code:	WQMFKA	Issuing Agent:	Nita City, Nita
Ticket Number:	5996739313271	Issuing Agent:	3BA78/4076
Issuing Airline:	CARIBBEAN AIRLINES	IATA number:	66397478
Date Issued:	30May22	Invoice number:	483228
Customer Number:	2896768575		
Passenger:	Cheryl Tobias		

14JUN22   Caribbean Air CA 1066   Seat 15A

From: Nita City, Nita (Nita City Intern'l)   Departs: 730A   Business Confirmed

To: Fort de France, Martinique (FDF)   Arrives: 355P   Fare Basis: TC8BX

Not Valid Before: 14JUN

Not Valid After: 14JUN

19JUN22   Caribbean Air CA 3631

From: Fort de France, Martinique (FDF)   Departs: 1150A   Business Confirmed

To: Nita City, Nita (Nita City Intern'l)   Arrives: 820P   Fare Basis: TC8BX

Not Valid Before: 19JUN

Not Valid After: 19JUN

Form of Payment: Credit Card - Visa - Charged to Jeffrey Potter

Endorsement/Restrictions: Nonref/Change Fee Plus Fare Diff Applies/Valid US Only

Positive Identification Required for Airport Check-In

Carriage and other service provided by the carrier are subject to conditions of carriage, which are hereby incorporated by reference. These conditions may be obtained from the issuing carrier.

Nita Travel Company . . . Your Gateway to Fun in the Sun!

Exhibit 38

MARTINIQUE PRINCESS HOTEL BILLING STATEMENT JUNE 14–19, 2022

Martinique Princess Hotel
76 Rue de la Plage
Forte de France, Martinique

Name: Mr. & Mrs. Jeffrey Potter   Guests: 2
Address: 4920 Thorndale Avenue   Room: 1370
             Nita City, Nita

Arrival: 6/14/22   *Departure: 6/19/22*

Date	Description	ID	Ref. No.	Charges	Credits Balance
6/14/22	Room/Deluxe Suite	MRC	1370	325.00	
6/14/22	I. Room Tax	MIT	1370	29.65	
6/14/22	City Occup. Tax	MOE	1370	10.98	
6/14/22	Room Service	MCH	1370	48.19	
6/15/22	Room/Deluxe Suite	MRC	1370	325.00	
6/15/22	I. Room Tax	MIT	1370	29.65	
6/15/22	City Occup. Tax	MOE	1370	10.98	
6/15/22	Masseuse	MAS	1370	80.50	
6/15/22	Masseuse	MAS	1370	80.50	
6/15/22	Room Service	MCH	1370	28.99	
6/15/22	Room Service	MCH	1370	158.90	
6/16/22	Room/Deluxe Suite	MRC	1370	325.00	
6/16/22	I. Room Tax	MIT	1370	29.65	
6/16/22	City Occup. Tax	MOE	1370	10.98	
6/16/22	Day Spa	MSG	1370	125.29	
6/16/22	Day Spa	MSG	1370	60.13	
6/16/22	Room Service	MCH	1370	33.48	
6/16/22	Laundry Services	MLS	1370	71.17	
6/16/22	Boutique	MBB	1370	148.75	
6/16/22	Room Service	MCH	1370	48.30	
6/16/22	Champagne Cruise	MCC	1370	198.45	
6/16/22	Champagne Cruise	MCC	1370	198.45	

6/17/22	Room/Deluxe Suite	MRC	1370	325.00
6/17/22	I. Room Tax	MIT	1370	29.65
6/17/22	City Occup. Tax	MOE	1370	10.98
6/17/22	Room Service	MCH	1370	68.90
6/17/22	Tarot Card Reader	MTR	1370	51.50
6/17/22	Masseuse	MAS	1370	80.50
6/17/22	Room Service	MCH	1370	62.99
6/17/22	Day Spa	MSG	1370	75.22
6/17/22	Flower Show	MFB	1370	31.00
6/17/22	Room Service	MCH	1370	79.42
6/17/22	Room Service	MCH	1370	108.14
6/17/22	Movies	MOV	1370	15.00
6/18/22	Room/Deluxe Suite	MRC	1370	325.00
6/18/22	I. Room Tax	MIT	1370	29.65
6/18/22	City Occup. Tax	MOE	1370	10.98
6/18/22	Day Spa	MSG	1370	28.68
6/18/22	Room Service	MCH	1370	43.10
6/18/22	Island Tour	MCL	1370	58.33
6/18/22	Island Tour	MCL	1370	58.33
6/18/22	Room Service	MCH	1370	61.30
6/18/22	Champagne Cruise	MCC	1370	198.45
6/18/22	Champagne Cruise	MCC	1370	198.45
6/19/22	Room Service	MCH	1370	38.95

$4,304.52

I agree that my liability for this bill is not waived and agree to be held personally liable in the event that the indicated person, company, or association fails to pay for any part or the full amount of these charges.

Thank you for being our guest at the Martinique Princess Hotel.